Steam and Steel
An Illustrated History of
SCUNTHORPE'S RAILWAYS

By
Bryan Longbone

IRWELL PRESS ≋≋≋

The Borough of Scunthorpe and the local iron and steelworks, mid-1950s. Essentially, the whole of the township south of the railway is post-1918 growth. The iron and steel industry is at its peak of activity due to the post-Second World War boom. At this date much mining of local iron ore was undertaken further north, beyond the map border. The iron and steelworks dominated the area, in more ways than one. Good job the prevailing winds were westerly...

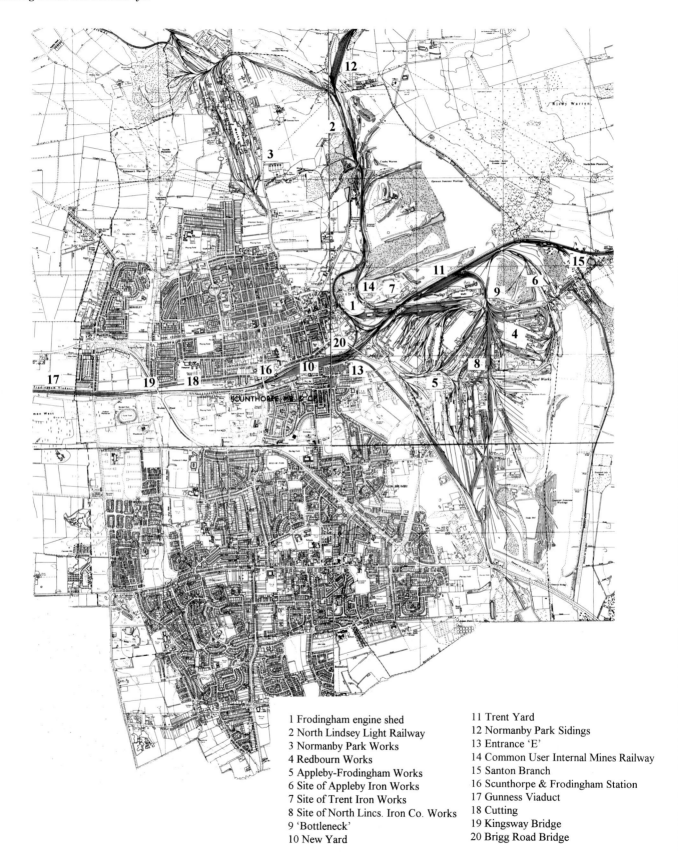

1 Frodingham engine shed
2 North Lindsey Light Railway
3 Normanby Park Works
4 Redbourn Works
5 Appleby-Frodingham Works
6 Site of Appleby Iron Works
7 Site of Trent Iron Works
8 Site of North Lincs. Iron Co. Works
9 'Bottleneck'
10 New Yard

11 Trent Yard
12 Normanby Park Sidings
13 Entrance 'E'
14 Common User Internal Mines Railway
15 Santon Branch
16 Scunthorpe & Frodingham Station
17 Gunness Viaduct
18 Cutting
19 Kingsway Bridge
20 Brigg Road Bridge

Contents

ACKNOWLEDGEMENTS

Railway research requires going back to original sources and coming to one's own conclusions. The sources are varied: South Humberside Area Record Office, Public Record Office (Kew), Scunthorpe Museum, Humberside Libraries, East Midlands Regional Record Office of British Steel plc and the Archives of the Great Central Railway Society. Many thanks to the staff of these bodies. The conclusions arrived at are often the result of sessions at the Workers' Educational Association class on South Humberside Railway History, but they bear the point of view of the author. Some 240 hours of talks, discussions and constructive discourse over the past twelve years, with little repetition, must, and has generated much interest. The author publicly thanks past and present participants for their perseverance and patience. Hope that the courses were worth the money, lads.

Contact with local railwaymen, all now retired and some now deceased, has been exceptionally rewarding, in many ways. The friendliness of these gentlemen has been matched by their informative reminiscence and the fascination of their working lives. Jim Allison, Les Amery, David Baker, Fred Coupland, Fred Digby, George Fussey, Fred Hallam, Len Jacklin, Bill Leeman, Ernie Pacey, Ellis Peckett, Les Smith and Walter Scott, along with several others, have been of valuable assistance. Many thanks to all and their families for the visits.

On a personal level I must acknowledge the understanding and kindness of my wife, Carol, on my frequent disappearances.

Roy Grimston has been truly helpful in supplying photographs. It seems the lure of the 'main line' overcame many a photographer over the years, and not many ventured into North Lincolnshire. David Davies at British Steel plc has also been very generous with his assistance. Photographs have been utilised from a variety of sources; many thanks go to the people concerned and they are identified where appropriate. The signal box diagrams are the work of John Foreman. In addition, sincere thanks are due to David Jackson for 'chewing the fat' on many occasions. Finally John Oxley is to be thanked for answering my persistent queries with regard to yard operation and so on.

In conclusion, the author would like this volume to stand as a memorial to his maternal grandfather. George Pettit started on the Great Central Railway at New Holland during 1919, transferred to Keadby shed and after the move to Frodingham finished in 1964. If only the job had not worn him out; mind you, he was a bugger for overtime.

First Published in the United Kingdom by
IRWELL PRESS 1996
P.O.Box 1260, Caernarfon, Gwynedd, LL55 3ZD
Printed in Huddersfield by The Amadeus Press

To the west of Scunthorpe the former Roman Road, Ermine Street, runs northwards from Lincoln to the Humber Bank at Winteringham. 63653 is about to cross this virtually straight road, at Appleby station in the early 1960s. The train is either empty coal out of Immingham Dock or foreign iron ore from the same site. The down platform is hidden behind the train which is about to attack Santon Bank on its way to Frodingham. Photograph R.E. Grimston.

Trent Iron Works loco line up, sometime between 1903 and 1920. No.2 (left foreground) is of unknown origin, ditto No.3 (right foreground) but No.5 is an 0-6-0ST, a Hudswell Clarke of 1903. A new No.3 was purchased in 1920 but it is not the loco pictured. Answers please to the author. Photograph D.G. Stark Collection.

INTRODUCTION

A Frodingham banking engine and what a sight and sound to behold, one which really stirs the memory. A splendid side view of a Yorkshire Engine Co. Austerity tank which is just easing off from banking an internal App-Frod ironstone train, up from Trent Remine in the early 1960s. This latter line ran approximately where the present coal handling plant is situated. The locomotive is ore mining branch No.14. Photograph R.E. Grimston.

This north west portion of Lincolnshire, with the River Trent as a western barrier, the Humber to the north and little of consequence in the way of major villages and agricultural wealth, was not high on the railway speculators' agenda. During the 'mania' years schemes were announced but these skirted the edges, mainly on a north-south axis in the race to Hull and points further afield. The east-west route of what became the Manchester, Sheffield & Lincolnshire Railway ran along the southern boundary, from Gainsborough through Brigg to New Holland and Grimsby. Another river formed an eastern limit, the canalised River Ancholme. In addition, and unlike the south of the county, the terrain from the Trent valley through to Barnetby boasts two principal escarpments, both running north to south. So if anyone wished to construct a railway across, it would cost a packet.

But wealth there was to be tapped. The South Yorkshire Railway constructed a line alongside its own canal to Keadby (opened 1859) for coal traffic, to enter the busy waters of the Trent and Humber and gain the east coast. During this time a local landowner realised further potential on the Frodingham portion of his Appleby estate - Rowland Winn, son of Charles Winn of Nostell Priory near Wakefield. By a

happenstance, Rowland Winn discovered the family acres to be well endowed with ironstone. The family were not sufficiently well off to bear the full burden of cost of a railway and co-opted, amongst others, the Dawes brothers. George Dawes was an ironmaster late of the Black Country, working ironstone at Elsecar and Milton in south Yorkshire while William Henry Dawes looked after the finances. These two leased approximately 950 acres from the Winn family and eventually had an ironworks built on the Frodingham estate, midway between the Trent and the Ancholme, appropriately enough called the Trent Ironworks. In addition to this local smelting, ironstone was shipped out of the area. A narrow gauge system (including a gin-worked incline) was employed while the railway from the Trent at Keadby to Barnetby (Wrawby Junction) was being constructed. In these early years ore was carried away by means of both rivers but the Trent soon came to the fore. However, once iron production got under way in 1864 the half-finished swingbridge over the Trent at Keadby proved a boon and soon this was the predominant route. This Trent crossing was part of the South Yorkshire Railway extension from the Keadby line, over the river to connect end-on with the Trent, Ancholme & Grimsby Railway, itself constructed simultane-

ously from Gunhouse Junction through to Wrawby Junction near Barnetby. Local competition to the Dawes brothers soon sprang up, a further five ironworks coming into production over the next dozen years.

The principal advantage of what became the Frodingham ironstone field was ease of extraction of the iron bearing rock and the consequent cheapness of later metal production. The stone first worked was at or near the surface and easily obtained. In later years there was further re-mining of the beds, to reach the very thick regular seams beneath. The ore though, was 'lean' - that is, low in iron content. One advantage (not realised until later, after some explosive trial and error) was that the ore was self-fluxing; it already contained lime. The process benefited accordingly, for it was not necessary to carry additional tonnages of limestone into the area. The low iron content, however, demanded commensurately more fuel - coal and coke. This could be obtained conveniently nearby; some 25-30 miles to the west, on the Manchester, Sheffield and Lincolnshire Railway. Consequently the management of the MSLR and South Yorkshire assisted (through loans for its construction) an infant 'Trent Ancholme and Grimsby Railway'. The MSLR controlled the SYR after 1864 in addition to the line from

1

Two immaculately turned-out ore mining Austerity tanks, at the head of an ironstone train. Bound for Appleby-Frodingham Works, they are passing Crosby Mines signal box on the North Lindsey Light Railway. At the rear of this scene is the 'Crosby Ironstone Mines' pit with tank engine in the loco siding. Photographed in the mid-1950s. Photograph D. Stark Collection.

Wrawby Junction to Grimsby Docks, and the future looked rosy for all concerned. The Trent and Ancholme remained nominally independent until 1882, in title that is, by which time all its stock had been purchased by MSLR interests. The MSLR was the power on the line from the beginning, contracted to operate the goods and passenger services. Charles Winn died soon after completion of the line, the family having sold the land to the railway company, of which his son, Rowland, was a director. The Winn family could then count the pennies received on each extracted ton of ironstone for many years after. Later this was effected through a company under the Winns' umbrella entitled the Frodingham Ironstone Mines Co., which sold stone locally and to outside iron smelters.

It was soon common knowledge that ironstone lay elsewhere in the district and smelting concerns such as that belonging to Charles Markham of Staveley desired access; Rowland Winn wished to retain his monopoly and naturally imposed a charge, or wayleave, on any stone which would pass from 'outside' across his land to the Trent and Ancholme. This burden of cost added on to the 'outside stone' rendered it uneconomic. Rowland Winn continued to supply a restricted tonnage rather than see the area opened up to all-comers. In a 'flanking movement' Edward Watkin, Chairman of the MSLR, with the support of various Derbyshire and Nottinghamshire-based ironmasters, ob-

tained Parliamentary sanction for a branch to a proposed mine on the Santon estate of Lord Yarborough. This was not a success, for the mine was a deep shaft and the price of iron collapsed during 1873, only a year after permission was received.

A precursor to what became the North Lindsey Light Railway was privately mooted by Rowland Winn during the mid-1880s. Titled in various correspondence as the 'Frodingham & Humber Wharf Railway', this was an attempt by Winn (created Lord St.Oswald by the Tory government, in 1885) to escape the monopoly of the MSLR. It was suggested that ironstone and pig iron be moved along this proposed line to a pier at Winteringham on the River Humber, thereby avoiding taking it to Grimsby via the MSLR. Winn was in dispute with the railway at this time and even approached members of the boards of the Great Northern and the Great Eastern, to build lines to Frodingham to escape the monopoly erected by Watkin. The response of the MSLR was to lower the rates on such traffic to Grimsby - maybe that was the result Winn had wished for all along.....

The Light Railways Act of 1896 spawned proposals of local note of which one, the North Lindsey Light Railway, was the sole (local) example laid down. It was promoted in 1898 and loosely followed the plan of the earlier Frodingham & Humber Wharf Railway, Winn's effort of some dozen years earlier. The

second Lord St.Oswald, Rowland's son, was opposed to a passenger station within the town of Scunthorpe but under pressure he acquiesced, asking a sum of £12,000 for the land required by the promoters of the NLLR for the station site and adjoining sidings. This proved to be too expensive but a compromise was reached on the land purchase and an annual rent of £400 agreed for other property. Consequently, ironstone on the Normanby estate of Sir Berkeley Sheffield, north of Scunthorpe, could be taken through by rail to the Great Central Railway (as the MSLR had become in 1897).

To return to Watkins' failed effort, the now-dormant 'Santon branch', built with the intention of tapping ironstone on Lord Yarborough's estate - mentioned above. The Frodingham Iron & Steel Co. had secretly approached the board of the Great Central in the early years of the century asking for a decision as to a connection off the GCR to Holme, south of the town. Here the steel company was pondering the erection of a completely new iron and steel works. The reason for this drastic measure lay in new American methods of charging open hearth furnaces. By this means the process could be speeded up, was less labour intensive and would also increase output from larger furnaces - in other words more steel produced in a given period of time. Because this method of 'mechanical' charging entailed considerable structural alterations and a much larger layout, a new site was considered essential. This new method of charging was with pre-filled pans of solid material transferred across from the loading bay to the furnaces by a manned electric-powered loader, which could serve several furnaces. This loader ran on a trackbed passing along the front of the steel furnaces or, in the later case of John Lysaght's works at Normanby Park, suspended rather like an overhead crane. As this method of charging was the latest in technology and the Frodingham Iron & Steel Co. desired to be one step ahead of its British rivals, secrecy over the procurement of the American patent (held by the Wellman Company) was paramount. The railway company suggested an extension of the Santon branch southwards to Holme and very quickly proceeded to relay the moribund line. Permission to retain the land for railway use had to be renewed every ten years in Parliament but this had been allowed to lapse since the 1880s and the GCR was on thin ice. There was stiff opposition from Lords St.Oswald and Yarborough, but a way out seemed to come in the form of an agreement between the Frodingham Iron & Steel Co. and Lord St.Oswald. Nothing came of the venture though, for the ironstone at Holme was found to be poor in quality. The stone lying to the north of the town *was* found to be suitable and the so-called 'light railway' of the North Lindsey became a

fully fledged industrial line, in use for many years. A passenger service even operated from 1906, but ceased during 1925 through cost cutting by the LNER, in the face of local bus competition.

Over the years very extensive mining has occurred to the north and south of the original sites, which were close to the ironworks adjacent to the Trent and Ancholme Railway. This is very obvious to anyone travelling through by rail. Industrial rearrangements also came, in particular between the wars, with the result that a very great iron and steel producing centre grew up, principally based upon the elements of cheapness, noted above. The most serious disadvantage was the lack of a nearby market for this semi-finished steel. The cost of transporting bars, blooms, billets, ingots, slabs and sections (for description see Glossary) all added to the price. The Frodingham-based steel industry has grown and subsequently maintained itself while producers nearer the markets have succumbed - all the more impressive an achievement since all the ore is now imported the twenty or so miles from Immingham Docks.

The following account relates to elements of the story of the local railway which served the iron and steel industry. I use the past tense, through a personal bias on my part for the period of steam locomotive operation, for

which I can offer scant apology. Not only the locomotives but the structural aspects of the railway and works on the ground are referred to. In summary, this is how, in a period of some 70 years or so, a very large iron and steel producing area was served by a railway monopoly.

Finally, a word concerning nomenclature. Although the title of this volume refers to 'Scunthorpe' the term (until recent years) used by all railway people and by those connected with the iron and steel industry has always been 'Frodingham'. This has been adopted in general throughout the book, and the narrative proceeds only until about 1970, the end of steam operation coming during 1966. The output of the local iron and steel works were 'Frodingham-products' and the London North Eastern Railway engine shed of 1932 was termed in similar fashion. The parish of Frodingham contained for a long time the bulk of the local smelting works and virtually all of the local main line railway network. It was only in 1936, with the creation of the Borough of Scunthorpe, embracing the parishes of Crosby, Scunthorpe, Frodingham, Brumby and Ashby, that the modern name came to the fore. In industrial usage, 'Frodingham' took a long time to disappear, and nowadays it is increasingly a memory.

An eastbound goods train about to cross the Trent over the King George V bridge, with O4 63584 at its head. The redundant Harts siding (it ran down to Harts Feedstock site on the river bank) leaves the main line approximately at the end of the train and crosses the road into Keadby, by means of the bridge visible centre background. Photographed at Althorpe station in the early 1960s by R. Grimston.

Above. The only known photograph of the first Frodingham station. The reason for the bunting and well-dressed crowd is not the opening of the station but the dutiful welcome for Rowland Winn, on the successful outcome of his lawsuit against Lord Beauchamp (on a question of land in the adjoining parish of Brumby). Hail the conquering hero! It is 1867, a year or so after the station was open for passengers. The down platform is behind the photographer with the siding to the Frodingham Iron Works bearing off to the left. The building behind survived for over 100 years and latterly was the Yardmaster's office. The ballast is almost to the top of the rail level, a common feature of the nineteenth century. Brigg Road level crossing is at the end of the up platform, the gatehouse is visible behind the early semaphore signal. The up side platform and buildings were swept away with the goods yard extensions, the new station being on Alexander Road, the other side of the level crossing.

Below. Looking east from the old footbridge at Frodingham, towards the partially obscured station c.1910. The blast furnaces of the Frodingham Iron & Steel Co. are central with the melting shop chimneys belching forth. The new Frodingham Estate, built for Rowland Winn during the 1870s, is on the right hand side of the railway. The site of the later LNER yard of the 1920s lies opposite. A former MSLR 0-6-0 is on the down main on a stopping goods with the two Midland Ironstone sidings adjacent. Photograph D. Parker Collection.

Chapter One

RAILWAY TRADE AND RAILWAY TRAFFIC

The story of the railways of Frodingham cannot be separated from the developments on the ironstone field and the associated iron smelting plants. Within fifteen years of the Dawes Brothers commencing construction of the Trent Iron Works in 1860-61 no less than five additional separate plants had been erected, all of them producing iron by 1876. The table charts the rise and fall of these local works. Of course numbers by themselves do not mean a great deal; the nineteenth century furnaces were small affairs and typical of 400 or so throughout the country, and they were subject to almost continuous rebuilding, enlargement and integration. By 1960 the output of the small number of large blast furnaces at three sites was many times that of the large numbers of relatively small turn-of-the-century affairs. Technical progress achieved much from about 1900 and the output of pig iron and steel rose considerably, albeit with hesitant steps, as the advantages of this Lincolnshire site were realised during the Great War of 1914-18. This is not to say there were no lulls in production; the General Strike and the Depression both made their mark, but not so acutely as at other iron and steel centres. All this bore directly on railway traffic and operation.

The earliest known ironstone output from Frodingham went to diverse locations, in at least one case reflecting the ownership of the site involved - the Trent Works, for instance, in the charge of the Dawes brothers, supplied their other works at Elsecar, in south Yorkshire. Local stone was given trial at various ironworks, in the Black Country at Tipton, Deepfields and West Bromwich; to North Staffordshire at Talk o' the Hill, Stoke on Trent and Shelton; in Lancashire at Darwen and Ditton; Yorkshire at Castleford, Hazelhead, Thorncliffe, Grimesthorpe, Parkgate and

BLAST FURNACES AND WORKS AT FRODINGHAM													
		Number of blast furnaces											
	First made	1870	1880	1890	1900	1910	1920	1930	1938	1945	1950	1960	1990
Trent Iron Works	1864	3	7	6	6	3	3	3	-	-	-	-	-
Frodingham Iron Co.	1864	3	4	3	4	4	8	8	8	10	8	4	4
North Lincs. Iron Co.	1865	1	4	4	4	2	3	3	-	-	-	-	-
Lindsey Iron Co.	1875	-	2	2	-	-	-	-	-	-	-	-	-
Redbourn Hill Coal & Iron Co.	1875	-	2	2	4	3	4	4	4	4	2	3	-
Appleby Iron Co.	1876	-	2	3	4	4	*	-	-	-	-	-	-
J. Lysaght Ltd	1912	-	-	-	-	-	4	5	5	5	4	4	-

*The Appleby Co. had been absorbed by the Frodingham Iron & Steel Co. by this date. See increase in figure for the latter.

The Frodingham & Scunthorpe station signal box and footbridge, sometime prior to the Great War. A local carrier and station staff pose for the camera - the horse-drawn omnibus worked to Scunthorpe 'to and from Great Central Railway' as advertised. 'Spavin' was, and still is, a well known local name. Photograph Scunthorpe Borough Museum.

Frodingham Goods Yard and Sidings, 1907 or later. The blast furnace of the Frodingham Iron & Steel Co. stand immediately beyond, with the running lines in between. The eastern curve to the North Lindsey Light Railway bears right across the foreground. Photograph Scunthorpe Borough Museum.

Leeds and at Middlesbrough, Durham and Newcastle. All these places received stone in varying quantities from the mid-1860s, for a decade or so. Some stone flows became well-established, the supply to Parkgate in particular continuing for many years .

As stone was being sent out of the district, Frodingham pig iron was also finding markets. In the nineteenth century much of it was destined for the puddling furnaces of the West Midlands but with the very widespread working of pig iron into forge and foundry products throughout the country, the Frodingham stuff travelled widely, on the strength of its quality, price and cost of transport. Quality was 'average' and the cost of production the lowest in the country but transport costs rose once the iron moved beyond south and west Yorkshire, Lancashire and Derbyshire. The MSLR was forced to quote low rates due to river/canal competition in most of these zones but Frodingham iron, through its very low mining and smelting costs, could often bear longer distance railway rates. The figures tell their own story; annual production of pig iron rose from 31,000 tons in 1870 to 350,000 tons during 1900.

Incoming raw materials were additionally required, chiefly in the form of coal and coke, an expensive commodity for the Frodingham iron producers as none was at hand, compared with many other locations. In order to forestall this, during 1865 Joseph Cliff, owner of the Frodingham Iron Works, bought a coke ovens in South Yorkshire. Poor quality coke resulted however; it was not a great success in the (then) blast furnace operations but against this, transport costs from south Yorkshire were about 4/- per ton cheaper, compared to much better quality blast furnace coke from Durham. Some comparative figures:

South Yorkshire
Denaby Main, coke. 31 miles 1s10d per ton = 0.7d per ton mile
Wharncliffe Silkstone, coke. 40 miles 2s2d per ton = 0.65d per ton mile
Durham
Hedley Hill, coke. 121 miles 5s10d per ton = 0.58d per ton mile
Lintz Green, coke. 138 miles 6s3d per ton = 0.54 per ton mile

During the 1870s it was found that the lower Barnsley seams gave good quality coke if mixed with a Durham supply. The coke ovens built during the 1880s at Mitchell Main, Wharncliffe Woodmoor, Carlton collieries and, during the 1890s, Wharncliffe Silkstone, supplied and relied upon the Frodingham market. South Yorkshire coke continually improved in quality and with the newly-opened collieries and ovens coming into production soon after (nearer to Frodingham) the stuff became even cheaper to transport. By 1907 Durham coke was nearly eclipsed. A new plant was laid down by John Lysaght in 1912, and its annual coal supply of 156,000 tons came from Brodsworth, Maltby and Askern collieries which were within 25 miles of Frodingham. The other works at Frodingham bought more coal and coke on the open market. Durham coal was resorted to once more in later years (after World War Two) at the Redbourn site as a constituent in a 'mix' of coals, to produce quality blast furnace coke on site.

After a helter-skelter time of trial and error, it was found that the local ores produced continuous and better iron with the addition of ores from the East Midlands, rich in silica. Thus from about 1870 ironstone was also brought to Frodingham, from South Lincolnshire (Monks Abbey and Greetwell) and from the Northamptonshire field around

A postcard view (taken about 1907-1912) from the top of the blast furnaces of the Frodingham Iron & Steel Co., looking along the Station Road. The GCR goods yard is prominent in the foreground with a panoply of LNWR, GWR, MR, GSWR, GER, GNR and LYR wagons - but no obvious GCR examples. Beyond is the North Lindsey Light Railway terminus platform with attendant coaching stock. The sidings and junction with the GCR trail to the right. The station area was the 'frontage' land expensively purchased from Lord St. Oswald. Photograph Scunthorpe Borough Museum.

Gunness Viaduct to the west of Frodingham, where the line rises at 1 in 93 from the Trent Valley. Built entirely of brick, there being no suitable local stone but plenty of clay, the piers stood on matting in the absence of a hard rock base. What looks to be a GCR Class 8A 0-8-0 'Tiny' is at the head of a long train - the banking pilot can just be seen. The viaduct had a severe speed restriction, and its conversion to an embankment was deemed a cheaper option than rebuilding - the line in the foreground, crossing 'Scotter Road' (now much wider and busier) belongs to the contractor, dating the scene as late 1910/1912. Photograph B. Longbone Collection.

Wellingborough. From the chemical point of view this improved blast furnace working and iron yield and set the stage for future practice, until the 1970s.

The Manchester, Sheffield and Lincolnshire Railway was 'customer-friendly' during the nineteenth century, as events bore out. It charged a 2/- per ton through rate from all south Yorkshire collieries to Frodingham from the 1870s and only litigation during the next decade upset the pattern. One outcome was that, almost whatever the distances involved, a market for coke could be found at Frodingham - which benefited iron production. Separate rates however, came into practice once a prolonged legal wrangle with the Denaby & Cadeby Coal Company was settled against the MSLR.

Much of the Frodingham pig iron during the 1890s was being sent via Grimsby to the east coast of Scotland in order to satisfy the iron consuming industries on the Clyde, demand there outstripping local supply. By 1896 the MSLR was allowing Frodingham producers a rebate of 1/- per ton to Grimsby on 100,000 tons of forge iron in order to promote the traffic and reduce stocks at Frodingham; it was a period of low demand and decline in production and the recently formed Lincolnshire Ironmasters Association, a combination of local iron-producing firms, put pressure on the railway for concessions on such traffic. Similar quantities were rebated in 1897 and in 1898 for the same reasons but at 1/6 per ton, again to assist production at the ironworks.

A specific insight into the trade is available for 1897, when C.T. Smith, the Goods Manager of the MSLR, requested that the Frodingham firms shipping pig iron bound for the Monks Hall works at Wigan 'proceed via Glazebrook and Ambers Wood rather than via Ardwick and the London, North Western Railway'. This was so that the 'whole distance rate' would apply and the MSLR would get a greater payment. Another destination crops up during 1898, Messrs. Pearson & Knowles Coal & Iron Co. of Warrington receiving pig iron from the North Lincolnshire Iron Co.

By 1899 further transport inducements to the Frodingham iron producers were apparent. A total of 425,000 tons was spread over several years at a 'special total rate' through Grimsby including a sea rate to Antwerp and Rotterdam for pig iron of 4/- per ton - on GCR vessels, of course. The total pig iron traffic for all destinations, home and foreign, through Grimsby for the years 1899 to 1909 was close on 800,000 tons.

From 1896 a new problem was troubling the ironmasters. For whatever reason, the local firms persistently complained of a shortage of wagons. Possibly this was due to the expansion of trade, catching up on the railway company when it was spending money on the London Extension. Three years later, with little satisfaction from the GCR, the ironmasters arranged an interview with Charles Steel, the General Manager of the Great Northern Railway, in the vain hope of inducing that company to extend its system to Frodingham.

Large tonnages benefited the iron traders at Frodingham as well as the GCR. The lower than normal rate on pig iron to Grimsby and beyond helped to maintain production, which kept coke and coal in demand at Frodingham and in both cases the railway obtained and maintained traffic where instead a reduction or run-down might have occurred. These lower rates were 'theoretically illegal' - whatever that might mean - no doubt such practice was part and parcel of general railway operation during depressed circumstances. This did not prevent local ironmasters asking for cheaper coal rates from south Yorkshire on occasions; when coal prices rose, transport rates did too,

The well-known firm of railway contractors, Logan & Hemingway, undertook the job of embanking the Gunness Viaduct. 'Muck' trains were worked from the main line at Gunhouse Junction, alongside the structure to an elevated position while the temporary line at the bottom brought infill dug from land adjacent to Frodingham cutting, specially purchased by the GC. The point shown here is half-way down the viaduct, on the northern side, where an opening was left (at the request of Lord St. Oswald) to maintain access for one of his tenants. It is now utilised by the underground water mains supplying the Iron and Steel Works from the River Trent. Photograph F.D. Smith Collection.

The first public passenger train having arrived at Winteringham, July 15th 1907. This village was one of the two termini, the other being Whitton on the North Lindsey Light Railway, adjoining the Humber Bank. The former MSLR 0-6-2T would be a Keadby engine. The platform still remains, albeit surrounded with farming paraphernalia. Photograph Scunthorpe Borough Museum.

for the railways also consumed coal. This then affected the iron producers in the form of higher transport costs. Generally requests for lower rates were resisted by Sir William Pollitt, the General Manager of the MSLR/GCR, though during the dozen or so years from 1895 it has been estimated that as much as 25% of pig iron output at Frodingham was subsidised by rebates - a not inconsiderable proportion, but to the satisfaction of all parties. It

must be emphasised that the various rebates listed above were of prime importance; if they were not resorted to the local iron and steel industry may have gone under and the railway company would have lost, in the end, enormous revenue.

The Frodingham Iron Co. commenced steel production in open hearth furnaces during 1890, changing its name then to the Frodingham Iron & Steel Co. It started off with steel billets but, find-

ing this market difficult to break into due to cheap imports, soon after 1900 commenced rolling steel sections, for construction purposes - though quantities were small. Other materials, including refractory bricks (for lining the steel furnaces) and 'galli' (foreign) ore, were brought into the area. This latter was ore of high quality, used in the basic open hearth steel process, and was imported through the Humber from places as diverse as Spain, Sweden, Brazil, North Africa, France and Newfoundland - yet further traffics for the GCR.

A newcomer into the Frodingham steelmaking stakes entered the field from 1906. At this date the south Wales and Bristol firm of John Lysaght Ltd. started surveying for a 'green field' or virgin site, adjacent to the newly laid North Lindsey Light Railway. This was upon land to the north of Frodingham, belonging to Sir Berkeley Sheffield (a director of the GCR from 1909 to 1922). Iron and steelmaking commenced in 1912 with this firm rolling sheet bar and billets for south Wales. The company intended to ship its products via the NLLR out of Winteringham Haven, on the Humber, but the GCR offered special rates to attract the Lysaght traffic via Immingham Dock to South Wales. This was the cheapest method for many years, until Flixborough Wharf was opened by Lysaght on the banks of the River Trent in 1938. The rail haul to Newport was rated at 10/6 per ton but an alternative triangular trade became established. Three coasters were chartered to move 4,000 tons of tinplate bars weekly to Newport at 6/- per ton. From south Wales coal was shipped to Normandy, in northern France, from where iron ore (from Caen) was carried to the Normanby Park works of J. Lysaght. Richer in iron with less phosphorous, this ore was more conducive to efficient furnace practice, and was added to the locally produced stone. Another south Wales connection was formed during 1908 when control of the Redbourn Hill Coal & Iron Co. passed into the hands of the Cwmfelin Steel & Tinplate Co. Redbourn commenced making steel slabs soon after the Great War and supplied tinplate bars to a variety of works in South Wales controlled by the Thomas family. In this way trainload steel traffic from Frodingham to south Wales originated, up the London Extension of the GCR and on to the Great Western Railway at Banbury.

The remaining iron producing firms (North Lincolnshire Iron Co., Appleby Iron Co. and the Trent Iron Co.) at Frodingham were still in operation during these changes. The Trent Iron Co. was owned by a Birmingham concern, with the North Lincolnshire Co. controlled by Stewarts & Lloyds from 1922 to 1931. In the early years of the century the Appleby Iron Co. had a set-to with Lord St.Oswald over the quality and supply of ironstone supplied by the latter, with the

A former MSLR class 6C 0-6-0 in the 400 series at Scunthorpe station, on the North Lindsey Light Railway. The engineman is enjoying the attention of the camera - despite his grimy clothes, his boots are shining. This engine would have been based at Keadby and is one of those 'maids of all work', the 'Jumbos'. Passenger services on this light railway were discontinued by the LNER in the mid-1920s, a cost cutting measure in the face of local bus competition. However, in pre-Great War days it seems to have been well patronised. Photograph Scunthorpe Borough Museum.

result that the works were closed down from 1910. The predominantly Scottish owners disposed of it to the Frodingham Iron & Steel Co. and both concerns became part of the United Steel Co. (Sheffield-based) after the Great War.

To return to the railway and its operation during the GCR period - as we have seen, up to 1911 there were wagon shortages and rate problems and the five years from 1906 was a period of constant complaint to the GCR regarding shortages of stock. Frequent correspondence between the GC General Manager, Sam Fay, other sections of the GCR and the Ironmasters Association produced no resolution of the problem. From the GCR annual accounts of this period cost reductions were being put into place due to depressed trade, but when matters improved the wagon shortfall continued. Other factors, such as demurrage, may have contributed. It also must be remembered that the GCR had a monopoly of the area and its trade; moreover it did not have the spur of competition, pressing to upgrade the services and facilities.

Up to 1906 the railway allowed a variety of rebates to operate on pig iron traffic through the port of Grimsby, continuing the process outlined above. The coastal rate for pig iron was 2/3d per ton and on this rebates of as much as 1/3d and as low as 9d were given to the Frodingham iron traders in order to promote commerce, reduce stocks and generally keep everything moving. Over the five years from 1901 to 1906 a total pig iron tonnage of 627,000 was rebated to some degree on the Grimsby route. Given that the total pig iron made at Frodingham rose from 350,000 tons in

1900 to 560,000 tons in 1915, a fair portion of Frodingham production was, in effect, subsidised by the GCR. Whether or not it would have been produced in the first place without this assistance is a moot point.

Apart from John Lysaght, with its own coke ovens, the supply of coke proved to be a problem for other ironmakers in the area. A clearer 'snapshot' indication of forwarding locations for south Yorkshire coke is given for 1901, a year in which the Barrow Collieries and others in the vicinity were supplying a lot of open market coke to Frodingham. These collieries were on the Great Central system, south west of Dovecliffe. Similar day-by-day occurrences have cropped up in the record; during 1906 for instance the District Traffic Superintendent of the GCR at Doncaster, Mr. C.E. Jones, was informed of the shortage of locomotives for both coke and pig iron working at Frodingham, and that the local works sidings should be cleared earlier in the day, 'as was done previously'. A year later severe congestion and subsequent traffic delays were being reported to the GCR, a recurring problem that was not alleviated until the late 1920s (and then only for a short while).

The summary below illustrates the extent of traffic to and from Frodingham. During 1922 about 550,000 tons of pig iron were produced by local firms along with 350,000 tons of steel. The coal, coke and ironstone inputs to Frodingham were also extensive, for there is a large volume reduction consequent on the production of iron and steel - in other words, the tonnages of incoming raw materials are much larger than the outgoing product. It all indicates the very extensive traffic that

the GCR carried to and from this area, both from within its own system and from elsewhere. It was truly the GCR 'Jewel in the Crown' as regards earnings for a single location. The 'summary of bulk traffics' was originally drawn up in 1922, to elicit from the soon-to-be created LNER its intentions regarding full train-loads of such traffic to and from Frodingham. A full train-load was defined in those days as one of 400 tons. There was, alas, little response from the LNER to this progressive thinking.

SUMMARY OF BULK TRAFFICS TO AND FROM FRODINGHAM 1922

Frodingham Iron and Steel Company:
-*coal from Thurcroft and Treeton Collieries (GCR)*
-*coke from Thurcroft and Orgreave (GCR)*
-*ironstone from Colsterworth (GNR, south of Grantham)*
-*pig iron to Steel, Peech and Tozer, Rotherham (GCR)*
-*pig iron to Samuel Fox, Deepcar (GCR)*

Richard Thomas and Company (Redbourn Works):
-*coal from Sharlston Colliery (LYR)*
-*steel to Monks Hall, Warrington and Wigan (LNW/CLC/GCR)*
-*pig iron and steel bars to Llanelly*

Trent Iron Company:
-*coke from Rotherham Main(GCR)*
-*ironstone from Loddington, west of Kettering(MR)*

John Lysaght Ltd (Normanby Park Works):
-*ironstone from the Lincoln area (GNR, GCR)*
-*pig iron and tinplate bars to Newport, Mon.*

North Lincolnshire Iron Company:
-*ironstone from Tinwell Sidings, Stamford (MR/GNR)*
-*pig iron to Stewarts & Lloyds of Mossend*
-*pig iron to Alfred Hickman, Bilston, Staffs. (GWR)*

Frodingham ironstone, to:
-*Sheepbridge Company, Derbyshire*
-*Leeds Steel Works*
-*Walter Scott Ltd. Leeds*
-*Yorkshire Iron and Coal Co., Ardsley*
-*large quantities to Partington Iron and Steel Works (Lancashire), Staveley (Derbyshire), Parkgate (S. Yorks.), Middlesbrough.*

Pig iron from Frodingham to:
-*Brymbo (N. Wales), Glasgow, S. Wales, Birmingham and Staffs..*

Ironstone to Frodingham from:
Northants, Stainby, Edmondthorpe, Wymondham, Tinwell, Colsterworth, Lincoln, Corby, Spratton, Finedon, Uppingham, Market Overton, and others.

Appleby station up platform and buildings during 1955. They no longer exist but for a long time this and Elsham station were the only representatives of original Trent, Ancholme & Grimsby Railway passenger stations built during the 1860s and little altered. At Appleby the platforms were staggered and the place frequently featured in the best kept station stakes. The 'Lincs' is added to reassure passengers that they are not in Westmorland. The gas lamps and shrubbery lend charm to the brick structure. Photograph H.C. Casserley.

Above. The King George V road and rail lifting bridge over the River Trent with the rolling lift span under test. An American concept, the massive counterbalance contained over 1,000 tons of slag and scrap rails, and the bridge was the largest of its type in the country. The control cabin is perched next to the lifting span (see the signalman's push bike) and, as a safety precaution, the road gates are closed to traffic. Just visible through the gap are several tank wagons on the former main line over the old bridge. Date unknown. Photograph Central Press/B. Longbone Collection.

Below. Steady Does It! A dramatic view of the rolling lift span of the Scherzer-designed bridge, a few feet from the level. This weighty span, along with the 1,000 ton counterbalance, was driven by electric motors through gearing, with appropriate braking systems. From inception the Achilles heel was that, in hot weather, the steelwork expanded such that the bridge could not close. The local fire brigade were frequently called out to hose it down - this did not go down well with the operating people at all.

Chapter Two

MAKING - DO

A basic, single road dead-end shed for one engine was constructed at Keadby, for the initial purpose of running services on the Doncaster to Keadby branch of the South Yorkshire Railway. With the advent of the local Trent, Ancholme & Grimsby Railway from mid-1864 and traffic associated with iron smelting at Frodingham, through train working was started from New Holland and Grimsby to points west on the MSLR; Keadby shed did not have a share in this, for the steady increase in materials to and from Frodingham was handled by engines associated with Grimsby and, in particular, Mexborough. The duration of an average engineman's shift, anything up to 18 hours, meant that workings to and from Frodingham could easily be accommodated from these two sheds. During these early years, roughly up to the turn of the century, Keadby's small complement of engines was engaged primarily as local pilots, both at Keadby itself and at Frodingham, including banking goods trains up the incline from the Trent Valley to Frodingham on the Gunness Viaduct. Later this involved the workmen's trains from Thorne to Frodingham. There were also local goods services between Barnetby and Doncaster and, in especial, coal trips to and from Hexthorpe.

Keadby shed and its workings were of minor status. From 1861 to 1881 only a handful of engine drivers and firemen resided in the Trentside villages and other staff such as boilersmiths increased only slowly, along with the various classes of labourers. No great upheavals occurred to upset the even tenor of life. This purely local state of affairs existed happily until changes were instituted at the end of the century - from then on, traffic relating to the iron and steel works increased at an ever greater rate; there was a rapidly rising population to match, and the needs in goods and services of these people, as well as local industry, rose proportionately. The number of pilots required at Frodingham

The primitive coal tippler of early Great Central days. Wharf and tippler were soon rebuilt, together with the Trent Bank alongside. Photograph B. Longbone Collection.

'Keadby and Althorpe' station on the former South Yorkshire Extension line from Keadby Junction to Gunhouse Junction. It was made redundant with the opening of the Scherzer lift bridge in 1916 and all that remains is the stationmaster's house. The station site is now a waste tip. The river and the swing bridge lie beyond the trees and the Harts branch bears off to the left beyond the crossing. Another local example of staggered platforms. Photograph B. Longbone Collection.

The King George V bridge, massive from the ground but possessing a slender elegance from the air. Photographed in the late 1950s with a WD 2-8-0 passing through on the down side. The stationmaster's house of the former Gunness & Burringham station is just visible on the far eastern bank. There is no trace of the original bridge although it lay only 60 yards south. Lord St. Oswald's wharf is visible on the left; it was approached by rail via a branch from Gunhouse Junction.

shed and fitting staff, in the guise of old coaching stock and a 'redundant gasometer'! Additional sidings were laid down around the shed and alongside the canal where space was available, but it got to the point where some thirty or so engines were on shed at any one time and upwards of *seventy* were stabled there at weekends, crammed into any available length of spare track both at the shed, alongside the canal and across Keadby Junction in the coal sidings. The shed itself had been built in 1859 and nearly all repairs and maintenance were carried out in the open. An extra engine pit was laid down on a road adjacent to the canal, for the first pit (outside the shed) was too small for the larger types then coming into use. Specifically this concerned the Class 8A 0-8-0 'Tinys'. Coaling was rudimentary, from the top of a coal staith by the canal, shovelled from wagon to tender. There was some roofing left, but the building was largely open to the elements; a turntable was put in at the junction about 1860 but anything larger than an 0-6-0 had to be turned at the North Lincoln Angle (local term for a triangle) adjacent to Trent Yard at Frodingham, some six miles away. Keadby might well have been the worst shed that ever existed - water was yet another problem, for there were no columns in the Frodingham locality until about 1912 and the source at Keadby Junction was the dirty canal nearby. Priming of engines and subsequent washing-out of boilers was a major problem and it was usual for tenders to be topped up before visiting the area. Good quality water was to be had at Barnetby and it is known

all but doubled and more of the through goods trains were detaching and attaching at Frodingham Goods Yard. The traffic in coal through Keadby, to the Trent vessels, was also increasing and the GCR realised that present and future traffic levels in the area required the establishment of an engine shed at Frodingham. There were active negotiations for a site from 1904 at least, but local circumstances

mitigated against such an undertaking; the available land was all tied up in ironstone leases and the railway authorities were finding that it would be necessary to pay for any ironstone underlying such land. Consequently any asking price was far too high for the GCR's liking.

The basic facilities at Keadby had to suffice for a while longer and make-shift arrangements were instituted for

One of the river piers being demolished on the 21st June 1920. A keel is alongside and behind are two of the concrete supports raised from the river bed. On the Althorpe bank is the brand new vegetable oil works. The substantial residence opposite may have been the bridgemaster's house. Work was delayed for a period due to strike action and it is said that bits of cast iron formerly making up the bridge were laid up for a while on the eastside river bank, prior to sending them to the Frodingham Steelworks. The Althorpe & Keadby station is in the background, right hand side. Photograph Great Central Railway.

MSLR with (occasionally) the later addition of a more powerful and up-to-date 0-6-0 to handle coal from Hexthorpe to the Trent Spout. With ironstone being worked from Frodingham to ironworks in the Staveley and Chesterfield area, 0-6-2 goods tanks worked regularly out of Keadby and similar engines handled the passenger services on the North Lindsey Light Railway, from its opening in 1906. The principal Keadby type was the 0-6-0 goods, in particular Class 6C 'Jumbos' and Class 9 'Claddies'. With the production batch of Kitson-built class 8A 0-8-0s, this series ('Tinys') became regulars in the area and some were outshedded to Keadby from Mexborough. A small enamel plate lettered 'K' was fixed inside the cab. Trentside pilots were invariably 0-6-0Ts, usually Class 18T, with rudimentary braking. The Frodingham pilots were usually 0-6-0 tender engines. It is known that representatives of the Class 1B 2-6-4T 'Zeppelins' (or 'Crabs' as they were known elsewhere on the GCR) were tried on local goods but the crews experienced braking problems. The 'Director' boiler certainly had the power but there was little in the way of adhesion. Following this they were

A post-grouping view along the canal towards Keadby Junction - the engine shed is behind the sidings to the right. The keel is the 'Attercliffe' of Hull, wending its way to South Yorkshire. The near engine is a former ROD 2-8-0 with a former NER 0-6-0 in front; the cluster of locos beyond include a former MSLR 'Claddie' 0-6-0. Photograph E.W. Carter/ Gainsborough Public Library.

The King George V bridge opened in 1916 but with the Great War raging, there was no rush to demolish the swing bridge. It served as standby for a while until demolition commenced in the midsummer of 1920. Few details are known - though it seems to have been taken down piecemeal - witness the rigging on the bridge deck. The date is October 29th 1920.

that the taking of water from tenders (especially if the engine had come from the Sheffield district) by the locals for home use was a common practice. Piped water supplies did not exist in the area with only wells and run-off as a source. The 'big men' of Mexborough loco., who regularly lodged at Keadby, demanded and obtained a supply of water from 'home' parts. This was

regularly delivered in large cans, to Althorpe station, by any available train.

Details of Keadby's early engine complement can only be surmised but hints, at least, come from various sources. In the early decades, up to 1890 say, engines were primarily 0-6-0s and 0-4-2s of a wide variety of classes. Many were ex-South Yorkshire in origin, rebuilt by the

tried on banking duties up to Frodingham from Gunhouse Junction. Robinson 2-8-0s were visitors from the start but not in any great numbers, for there were no turning facilities. It was not until LNER days, when the ROD version became available in numbers, that these engines began their long association with Frodingham.

The Trent Spout at Keadby during the 1920s, with a Markham Collieries wagon tipping coal into the 'Brendonia' of Goole. The 'Acrity', an Everard vessel of London, is riverside awaiting loading with a keel between. The entrance to the canal is left of photograph. The coal tipper was steam powered from a small boiler nearby. The width of the river at high tide is notable; it was only some five miles or so from its confluence with the Ouse, forming the Humber. Photograph E.W. Carter/Gainsborough Public Library.

The type of engine most fondly remembered by former Keadby enginemen remained the 'Tiny'. Simple and rugged, with a boiler capable of being thrashed, it was just the ticket for the long and heavy but slow local goods trains. The 2-8-0 version proved ideal too, and had the same Robinson qualities.

When railwaymen gained the 8 hour day during 1919, engine crews at Keadby shed stood at about fifty, with a similar number filling the other grades at the shed. The shed foreman was a Sammy Hoole who came over from the fitting side at Mexborough. When prompted by devious fitters he was not averse to finishing off a fitting job himself. Six fitters were there in all, with one on the night shift. One or two worked 'as required' on 'stop-work', in other words, front end, valves and brakes. There were about fifteen cleaners per shift (two per day of 10 hours each), one boilersmith on days with another on night work. A tuber worked days, complemented by two washers-out. The day foreman was master over the cleaners and shed shunting, in addition to changing over the wash-out engines. His colleague on nights worked out the relief roster so that all the jobs arising were covered with engines and men. Dick Mawson was the shed clerk and one of

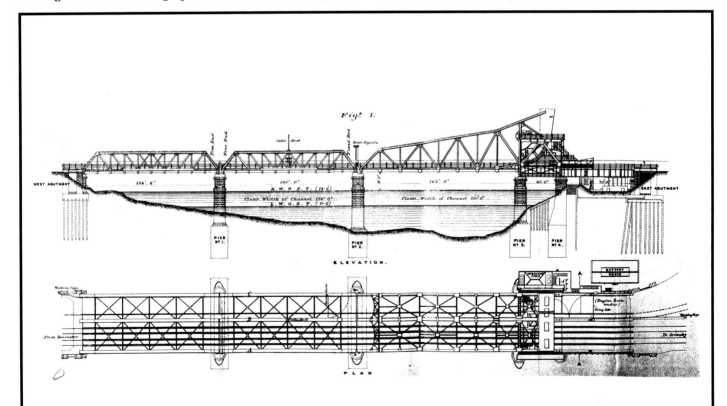

Figᵗ. 1.

ELEVATION.

PLAN.

General arrangement of the Keadby King George V bridge, opened for traffic in 1916. The GCR, over a dozen years or so, hesitated about replacing or rebuilding the earlier swingbridge. By 1909-10 a proposed deviation of the railway from Keadby through to Frodingham & Scunthorpe station was mooted. This entailed a new bridge spanning the river as a continuation eastwards of the branch into Keadby and a bridge similar to that finally built was put on paper. The Board of Trade objected that its location was too near the canal entrance. Soon after, the GCR was promoting another deviation line, but purely for the new bridge, some 60 yards north of the old. Some delay occurred in its construction due to steel shortages during the Great War. It was officially named the King George V bridge upon opening for traffic. A rolling lift bridge of the Scherzer design, it was an example of the GCR utilising the most modern thinking of the time. The Scherzer Co. of Chicago designed the structure in conjunction with the GC and Sir William Arrol & Co. of Glasgow built it. The bridge was but part of a grander scheme linked with the opening of Immingham Dock, the Doncaster Avoiding Line, Bentley Junction to Stainforth and Thorne Widening, the filling in of Frodingham Viaduct and the Barnetby to Brocklesby Widening, as well as Keadby Bridge, associated with the growth of dock traffic.

Two former MSLR class 6C 0-6-0 'Jumbos' with a westbound train on the Trent bridge. The protective 'Dolphins' for the bridge piers are very evident, and were erected in the earliest days of the 1860s, in order to lessen collision damage. The date is unknown but both engines appear to be sporting Robinson chimneys; the leading engine is possibly an assisting pilot over the Gunhouse Junction - Keadby Junction section. Photograph B. Longbone Collection.

his jobs was to make out the daily roster.

Below is the record of a typical Local Departmental Committee (LDC) meeting concerning railwaymen at Keadby engine shed. The LDC system was an outcome of the 1921 Railways Act, whereby joint meeting between local management and men ironed out grievances and settled minor local matters of routine.

Local Departmental Committee Meeting held at Keadby, April 17th 1923
Present:
Company side Mr. G.F. White(Chairman)
Mr. S. Hoole
Clerk W. Crossley (Secretary)

Employee side
Driver J.T. Ellis
Driver W. Jewitt
Coalman A.T. Rusling
Fireman V.C.J. Amery

ITEM 1
Several men have not received their annual supply of clothing, notwithstanding that they have made per-

The high and wide Trent seemed to make the old swing bridge appear larger than it was. It was in fact quite a spindly affair and by Victorian standards, cheaply built. This is the open bridge, seen from the east bank (looking south) on January 14th 1910. Gunness & Burringham station would be on the left bank, off picture. Note the bridge cabin semaphore indicating to non-existent river traffic that the swing span is open. Photograph Great Central Railway.

The interior of the then new Keadby Canal Junction signal box, erected in connection with the renewal of the canal bridge in 1926. This box replaced Keadby Junction and Canal East signal boxes as well as controlling the opening/closing of the canal bridge. The section of line is evident from the diagram. Equipment was supplied by the British Power Railway Signal Company. The control panel is to go to the National Railway Museum when the time comes and at present serves only for bridge and level crossing operations. Photograph B. Longbone Collection.

sonal application for same. *Matter in the hands of the Running Superintendent and will be put right as soon as possible.*

ITEM 2
Clothing for callers-up and barlayers; although personal applications have been made, they are still not to hand. *Suggest that the company provide mackintosh and leggings to loan to the man for calling-up in wet weather.*

ITEM 3
Referring to Mr. Crossley's visit to Keadby, 24th August 1922, re. bunker plates for Jumbos should be provided, this was done. Other engines of the same class are now stationed here, but are not provided with the plates in question. *This has been put in order.*

ITEM 4
Several Jumbo engines are without footstalls. *Jumbo engines are fitted with standard footboards and the Company cannot agree to alter them.*

ITEM 5
Existing links are not considered satisfactory. This committee suggests rearrangement and also recommends that three senior hands be appointed

to bank pilot between Gunness and Frodingham. *Agree to put the three senior men in separate links to work round on the banking pilot, rearrange the jobs in the links and equalise the number of men in the links.*

Signed G.F. White, W. Crossley, V.C.J. Amery.

Notes - the Jumbos were the former MSLR Class 6C 0-6-0s which had been associated with Keadby for many years. With the later influx of ROD 2-8-0s on to the LNER,

The only known photograph of engines on shed at Keadby. This dates from about 1928-29 with two Q4s and a J50 and two 'Poms-Poms' behind. The shed roof, or what remains of it, is behind and the North Soak Drain separates the shed and goods yard from the Keadby branch itself. Photograph R.S. Carpenter Collection.

these 0-6-0s did not last much longer. No photograph has come to light showing such an engine with a bunker plate (for reverse running) but this is not surprising, given the lack of local railway photographs. Sammy Hoole was Keadby shed foreman.

The years of the Great War dragged on, with government control until 1921 and the GCR was not about to spend money on the proposed new shed at Frodingham, though from the foregoing, it will be clear that it was desperately needed. The future was still uncertain - and further uncertainties arose from the Government withholding expenditure for such projects; endless correspondence and meetings came to nought. When the LNER was formed some of the hesitancy was ended but what money was available largely went on 'civil' works, rather than buildings for the 'Cinderella' running department. The LNER Act of 1925 did include a new shed at Frodingham but financial prudence prevailed and it was only with government financial assistance during the Depression that the shed was finally built, opening in 1932. It stood on the remains of the former Lindsey Iron Works on Dawes Lane; some thirty years had passed in which the ruinous 'shed' at Keadby had soldiered on, in extremely Spartan conditions alongside the canal, but the prospect now presenting itself 'up top of t'hill' was a state of the art, reinforced concrete structure. Nevertheless, appearances were slightly deceptive and the memory of Keadby lived on in conditions at the new shed, for the wind (and odours from the nearby iron and steel works) *'fair whistled through....'*

In later years the bridge was lifted much more for testing than for high masted river vessels. The weight of trains over the years had worn down the lifting span guide tracks with the result that the bridge was only lowered with difficulty. Note the flat, featureless farming landscape all the way to Yorkshire across the Isle of Axholme.

Left. An aerial view of Keadby and the Trent, taken from the top of Keadby power station about 1958. The canal enters the river from the west with the Keadby branch on its northern bank. The shed and goods yard were approached by the line deviating over the North Soak Drain (centre of photograph); the site of Keadby shed lies west of this. The Trent coal spout is visible on the bankside. Mid-distance the King George V bridge spans the river. A line of trees marks the progress of the Gunness branch from the junction to Gunness Wharf. A summer view - much stubble burning in progress.

Left. One more North American, this time in the shape of a 3-aspect upper quadrant power signal. Several were sited between Keadby Junction and Gunhouse Junction, on both lines. The system enabled a speedier movement over the river, given the frequency with which the bridge was raised. The only other example in Britain was one on the GW at Paddington. The GC installation was designed by the company's progressive signal superintendent, A.F. Bound, and manufactured by the British Pneumatic Railway Signal Co. This signal stands on the up line approaching Althorpe station with Hart's siding diverging left. The King George V bridge is beyond.

Below. A faded but rare view of a goods train from Frodingham, bound for South Yorkshire, close by the Stainforth & Keadby Canal just west of Crowle. The wagons are all coke empties with three belonging to the Appleby Iron Company. The locomotive is a double-framed 0-6-0. It is fascinating to see just how close the South Yorkshire Railway laid its Keadby line to its canal. The cottage is still there, some 100 or so years later, although the canal has been embanked. Photograph Scunthorpe Museum.

E.L.S. 12-22. ON THE CANAL, CORNOW BRIDGE, CROWLE.

Right. The main running lines just before the crossing of the Stainforth & Keadby Canal, on the west side of Keadby Junction. The former turntable pit is just visible (since filled and covered over) and the power station, built in the early 1950s, has now succumbed to explosives, ball and chain and the cutting torch. The three 350ft chimneys were a local landmark rising above the Trent flats. The signal bracket, electrically powered from Keadby Canal Junction signal box, controls the up line. The small arms on the left are non-block for the Keadby branch. 19th June 1961. Photograph R.E. Grimston.

Below. An English Electric Type 3 on a Frodingham-bound coal train in 1972, with the site of the Gunness & Burringham station goods yard in the foreground. The photograph is taken from the embankment of the old line over the swing bridge. The King George V bridge was constructed, along with the Keadby deviation railway, within the deviation limits of the former railway, so no Act of Parliament was required. The two railway houses still remain.

Above. As mentioned elsewhere, railway photographs of the Frodingham area during the LNER period are hard to come by. One example unearthed shows D6 5874 at Scunthorpe & Frodingham station with a down passenger train heading west. The year is 1937 - after May, for that is when 5874 came to Immingham shed from Gorton. 5874 is just one example of the former MSLR 4-4-0s of class D6 D7 and GCR D9 4-4-0s which were the mainstay of local passenger traffic.

Below. A rare, if much knocked-about, view of Frodingham & Scunthorpe station. It was built in the 1880s by the MSLR on Alexander Road, by a busy level crossing between Scunthorpe and some of the works. It went out of use by 1928 with the opening of the present (LNER) structure. O4 No.6347 is pausing at the up, Cleethorpes platform. The building design was repeated on a smaller scale, at MSLR stations in South Yorkshire. Photograph J.T. Wydale, Scunthorpe Borough Museum.

Chapter Three

TWENTY FIVE YEARS WITH THE LNER

At Frodingham as well as nationally, the iron and steel industry was much altered in structure and location during this relatively short period - the quarter century of railway 'grouping', from 1923 to 1948. The Great Depression of the early 1930s saw firms everywhere go under but by the middle of the decade, as conditions began to ease, a new pattern was established, remaining so through to the nationalisation of railways in 1948.

With the Trent Iron Company and the North Lincolnshire Iron Company disappearing, and the remainder consolidating with concerns outside Frodingham, there was a healthier outlook for local products. Only passing references to plant extensions will be noted - those which bear directly on the railway's operation. Improvements and increases in capacity were constantly being carried out, which meant that production at Frodingham was generally on the increase, with all that that implied for the LNER.

By 1935 a balanced state of affairs had been attained, whereby more steel than pig iron was being produced; tonnages as below:

Year	Pig Iron	Steel
1920	589,000	329,000
1925	548,000	410,000
1930	753,000	689,000
1935	861,000	1,085,000
1940	1,308,000	1,292,000
1945	1,039,000	1,099,000
1950	1,239,000	1,561,000

Virtually all the 'make' of pig iron was processed into steel, additions of scrap making up the difference. However a certain amount of cold pig iron was leaving for South Yorkshire to feed the 'cold metal furnaces' in steel melting shops. 'Cold metal practice' is where the entire quantity of materials charged into a steel furnace are melted down by oil or gas firing. 'Hot metal practice' is where the iron is added in the liquid, molten (1,400 degrees centigrade) state. Hence blast furnaces within easy distance are a prerequisite.

This hot metal practice ruled in the melting shops of the three local 'integrated' iron and steel works. All produced coke in ovens, smelted iron in blast furnaces, made steel in open hearth furnaces and rolled steel ingots to a semi-finished

condition, ready to be transported for finishing processes elsewhere in the country. In other words, Frodingham produced steel at the 'heavy' end. The 'light' end of production was where useable, saleable products resulted, though the Appleby and Frodingham works of the United Steel Co. did roll piling and sections (girders and so on) which were directly 'utilisable'. Obviously it was the LNER that gained in the transportation of this steel. The consolidation of steel production at the three integrated works was achieved before the outbreak of the Second World War. To the LNER fell the lot of coping with this burden, in the form of an endless series of goods and mineral trains.

The summary relating to 1922, at the end of Chapter One, held true (as far as the main flows were concerned) for some years after - a more detailed examination of the sources of coal, etc. is available for 1927 (below) but only in relation to the two ironworks within the Appleby and Frodingham complex and the supply of sundry materials to Normanby Park. At this date the Redbourn and Normanby Park works processed coal slack into coke with only the Appleby-Frodingham works

A former ROD O4, No.6287 on Frodingham shed, west end, on 23rd May 1937. Photograph W.L. Good.

An example of the much appreciated GC 'Tiny' - No.5153 on shed in 1937. The class was associated with the area for nigh on 50 years. Simple, sturdy, easy to maintain and drive, it suited everybody. By this time 5158 possessed a trimmed down steam dome and sported a replacement LNER chimney. It was a Keadby loco from GCR days and left Frodingham for Brunswick in 1943. Photograph W.L.Good/ W.T Stubbs Collection.

receiving large tonnages of coke. So, some 1927 traffics:

Frodingham Iron & Steel Co.- coke from Beighton, Hoylands, Barrow, Old Silkstone, Houghton, Wombwell and Rockingham (all on former Great Central in south Yorkshire).

Appleby Iron Co.- supplies received from the following collieries: Wath, Wharncliffe, Woodmoor, Barrow, Deepcar and Barnsley (all on former Great Central in south York-shire).

General supplies for the Frodingham and Appleby works - coke from Crigglestone and Rockingham Ovens; slack from Allerton Main (east of Leeds); hards from Bentley (north of Doncaster); washed dou-bles from Rossington (south of Doncaster); iron ore from Edmondthorpe (near Melton Mowbray); lime from Ambergate; coke and coal from New Monckton; coke and coal from Old Silkstone.

Material for Normanby Park - washed slack from Hatfield.

('Slack' - small, finely crushed coal; 'hards' and 'washed doubles' are coal grades).

At this date the Appleby works and Frodingham works were under the ban-ner of the United Steel Company; it was not until October 1934 that the term 'Appleby - Frodingham' came into use.

This list is not complete in materi-als or their origins, but it emphasises the extent of Frodingham-bound working by the LNER. Ironstone came in several times a day from the High Dyke branch, south of Grantham, in addition to the Northamptonshire ores. A train per day of ironstone also came from Holton-le-Moor on the Market Rasen - Lincoln branch. This latter was bound for Lysaght's works at Normanby Park. Con-ditions and quantities varied and were dependent upon the state of the iron and steel trade. Much of the south Yorkshire coal and coke traffic was handled through Wath Concentration Sidings with return empties from Frodingham worked back directly. This was a carry-over from Great Central days, initiated when Wath Yard opened during 1906-07. The intensive working of iron ore trains from the High

'Any old iron'. The 1930s procedure of unloading the dense, heavy foreign ore from ves-sels at Immingham Dock. Men in the hold filled each bucket by spade until about 20cwt-25cwt (yes it is dense stuff) was loaded. After lifting out by dockside crane it was deposited in the wagons on the adjoining quayside. Photograph A.E. Pool.

A Frodingham 'Zeppelin' - former GCR class 1B (LNER L1) No.273 (LNER 5273) on shed, May 1937. The nickname was a local term, elsewhere they were termed 'Crabs'. Examples were noted in GCR days at Keadby, originally on coal trains, but lack of braking power limited their use. They ended up on banking and other pilot turns at Frodingham before moving away prior to 1923. Some returned during the LNER period and worked the heavy pilot jobs - this particular engine was at Annesley in 1923 before going to Keadby, after which it had a spell at Immingham before moving on to Frodingham. The 'Star of the East' has been used on Immingham diesels in recent times, so maybe the star on 5273 is a symbol of some 50 years standing - other former GC engines have been noted with this embellishment. Photograph W.L. Good/W. Stubbs Collection.

Dyke branch, with return empties, was a principal feature both between the wars and for some years after 1945. In addition, ore from the Northamptonshire field was worked northwards by the LMSR to Swinton, near Mexborough, and from here forwarded by the LNER to Frodingham. Again this was a heavy traffic.

The following phrase - *'Special rate of 3d per ton off 2/11d per ton to liquidate stocks of pig iron, to check foreign competition, through Immingham and Grimsby...',* contained in a communication from the LNER authorities to the Ironmasters during 1931, began a two year episode which had similarities with events some 35 years earlier. Much correspondence between the LNER and the Ironmasters Association ensued but what follows is only a summary. It was, of course, kept under wraps at the time, the practice being illegal! Frodingham pig iron could not command a market in south Wales due to cheaper continental imports and it was this 'dumping' that prompted the LNER authorities to seek traffic and revenue by rate rebates on pig iron, which would be carried by coastal vessels loaded on the Humber. The rate by rail to south Wales at this time was 12/6d per ton and in a private discussion at the *Queens Hotel*, Leeds, between representatives of the LNER Goods Traffic Department and the Ironmasters, this rate was reduced by 1/5d per ton for Welsh and export pig iron. The management at the Normanby Park works of John Lysaght quickly saw ad-

vantages here in that it would assist in its traffic for south Wales and, in addition, allow exports to the USA through Immingham Dock. During this period of the early 1930s the LNER's idea was to disperse accumulated stocks of pig iron and start up out-of-blast (shut-down) furnaces. This was during the Depression and trade had seriously slumped - and

thus revenue for the LNER had declined. Lysaght became enthusiastic about this illegal venture whereby the firm could maintain production in this lean time, undercut its rivals (in other words gain illegal preference from the LNER) and continue at a higher level of production. The firm also wished to commence output at its newly built battery of coke ovens at

LNER class J11 'Pom-Pom' No.5304 in sparkling black at the western end of Frodingham shed. Photograph B. Longbone Collection.

Normanby Park, thus replacing 4,500 tons of coal brought in by the LNER with 7,000 tons per week of slack. This was in addition to a third blast furnace reinstated for the proposed North American traffic.

By January 1932 the special rates were being applied to these tonnages of pig iron:

Frodingham Iron & Steel Co.	
(United Steel Co.)	50,000 tons
Appleby Iron Co. (Utd. Steel Co.)	50,000 tons
North Lincolnshire Iron Co.	50,000 tons
John Lysaght Ltd.	50,000 tons
Trent Iron Co.	17,000 tons
Richard Thomas & Co.	
(Redbourn Works)	2,000 tons
Total	219,000 tons

These rates and tonnages applied to pig iron exported out of Immingham and Grimsby from the Frodingham-based works only. The USA-bound pig iron was included with these. These quantities were in the process of being delivered when in December 1932 a John Lysaght sister works, in Newport, south Wales, got wind of these rate reductions. The management at Newport was naturally enough anxious to have the same conditions from the Great Western Railway. The traffic concerned was tinplate bars from Normanby Park works to the Newport works, the latter desiring to have the claimed rate operated by the LNER, at 9d per ton of pig iron to 'a port 30 miles away' - Grimsby and Immingham. The 'public declared rate' from Normanby Park to Immingham was 3/10d per ton in trainloads of 800 tons including wharfage, cranage and slinging - a large difference indeed. The LNER offered its regrets to the local Ironmasters at this matter becoming public and, reluctant to ruffle feathers any further, hoped it would all go away. Persistence on the part of the GWR during 1933, however, forced the LNER to terminate the special arrangement, by reducing the rebate by steps over a period of fifteen months. This the local firms agreed to; demand in any case was picking up and import controls on steel had been introduced during 1932.

The post-Depression upturn in trade is reflected in 1936 figures for tonnages of imported iron ore through Immingham Dock bound for the Frodingham works. A total of 284,000 tons of foreign ore came in, transported to the various works by rail in trainloads of approximately 800 tons, an average of one per working day throughout the year. This was a very considerable increase over the previous few years and indicated a marked rise in local iron and steel output. This demanded more coke and more coal, leading to more train workings, more traffic and more profit for the LNER.

The co-operation between the railway and the Frodingham-based firms broke down on one occasion during 1935. The bar and strip mill at Whitehead Thomas was to be transferred from Tredegar in South Wales to a site on the Redbourn Works, in anticipation of Scandinavian orders through Hull and Goole, but the owners of Redbourn Works, Richard Thomas & Co., complained of there being no decrease in dock charges at these ports to assist the traffic. The firm declared that the Middlesborough iron and steel makers had a cheaper rate to Hull than did Frodingham via Thorne Junction. They wished also to have a reduction of the rail rate via Thorne Junction to these ports, for the traffic could not be shipped by the alternative route of New Holland. Nothing is known as to the outcome but as the Whitehead Thomas mill was duly laid down at the Redbourn site, some compromise must have been reached.

There were of course great difficulties encountered during the Second World War. Due to bombing and blackout, and the general congestion of the railways, it became next to impossible to take iron and steel to south Wales by rail in sufficient quantities. Some was shipped out of Manchester after arrival by rail from Frodingham, a route seventy miles by rail and 280 by water. Apart from the dangers of submarines, each journey took an age to accomplish and demanded a lot of labour - in terribly short supply by this time.

Mr. A. Pittwood, the Secretary of the Scunthorpe Traffic Committee, with the help of David Quibell, the local MP and J. Brooke, General Manager and Director of John Lysaght, suggested the use of a few vessels of 1,300-1,800 tons capacity, departing from Flixborough Wharf on the River Trent to travel to south Wales. The route taken thereafter was via the north of Scotland. This, it was suggested, would take less time and the proposal was supported by the LNER District Goods Manager, Mr. Duncan Gracie. The Ministry of Supply cancelled the Manchester route and the Scottish coastal route was proceeded with. At one period during the war over a quarter of Frodingham production was shipped in this unexpected fashion.

Increases in works capacity occurred at all the local firms during the 1930s but the principal construction phase was the building of a new iron works, coke ovens, and all the rest at Appleby-Frodingham. Two very large, American-inspired blast furnaces were completed just prior to the Second World War and with this and other smaller extensions elsewhere, Frodingham steelmaking capacity was, fortuitously, perfectly ready for war. Further extensions and enlargements awaited but did not take place until after the 1945 Labour Government was ushered in.

LNER D3 No.4309 on a back road on Frodingham shed, out of steam on 23rd May 1937. The engine had arrived at Frodingham shortly before this photograph was taken and proceeded thereafter to work a triangular local passenger diagram, going out from Scunthorpe to Barnetby with the morning Doncaster mail, working a stopping passenger train from Barnetby to Thorne and then returning with a workmen's train to Scunthorpe. In the evening the diagram was repeated. 4309 replaced withdrawn D7 (former GCR class 2 and 2A) engines on these duties and was in turn replaced by D2 No.4377. This is an unusual example of Frodingham hosting a passenger engine - such duties were normally undertaken by 'Pom-Poms' which more often than not were preferred to the 'foreigners'. Photograph W.L. Good/W.T. Stubbs Collection.

Chapter Four
THE LNER FOOTS THE BILL

onstruction of the Trent, Ancholme & Grimsby Railway upon land belonging (in the main) to the Winn family, combined with the east to west, strip-like nature of the property, within the parish of Frodingham, created problems in later years. The various works which developed in the twenty years from opening were adjacent to, or not a great distance from, the railway. As the major landowner, Rowland Winn wished to make money from his ironstone rather than that of neighbouring landlords, so a hodgepodge of sidings grew up, serving each iron works. Two focal points were to emerge - the Trent Down Sidings feeding the iron works of the Appleby, North Lincolnshire and Redbourn Hill companies, and the area to the west adjoining the works of the Trent and Frodingham Iron companies. (There was the nearby Lindsey Iron Works but this was in production only for a relatively short time). The trouble was that for the railway to increase siding capacity it had either to

pay considerable sums for land with underlying ironstone (in English law one pays for the underlying minerals) or wait for land to become available after the stone had been worked out. The MSLR preferred the latter option.

In north Lincolnshire, the MSLR exercised a regional monopoly and, secure in its position, expended little cash beyond that required for local necessities. History caught up with it though, for the Great War brought boom conditions to the iron and steel industry, and the railway was ill-prepared. For about 20 years previously the GC had contented itself with laying down the odd siding or two in piecemeal fashion, in particular at Trent Down Sidings (or Trent Yard of later years) and at the eastern end of this, termed 'the Angle'. But during the Great War it was increasingly pressed by local ironmasters to facilitate faster and easier train movements. Realisation dawned on the GCR management that something major had to be done to appease their clients and

though a scheme was duly put forward, it was to be taken up only some ten years on, under LNER auspices.

The GCR proposed a site a new station further west along the main line, at a spot in fact where the LNER was actually to open such a station, in 1928. The major difference was that the GCR October 1918 scheme included a large yard down the Midland Ironstone Branch on Brumby Common, this being south of the then passenger station on Alexander Road. Here a generous spread of sidings would serve the adjacent works of the Frodingham Iron & Steel Co. and the proposed Appleby Melting Shop and Plate Mill nearby. Access would have been to the south of the then works layout, along what later became North Lincoln Road.

Post-war uncertainties however, curtailed such prospects. The GCR 'had no money and no means of paying for the work' and saw it as a cost to be set against 'war measures'. 40% might thus be got from the government and the iron com-

An aerial, eastward, aspect of the whole of the new yard and railway, taken about 1958/60. The lines (the yards are divided into inwards and outwards) neatly bisect Scunthorpe, which rapidly filled in the original five separate parishes of Crosby, Scunthorpe, Frodingham, Brumby and Ashby. A local circus is encamped on the Manley Street playing fields, site of the GCR's proposed shed in the early 1900s - the LNER Frodingham engine shed is located at top left. Entrance 'E' (the former Midland Ironstone branch) bears off top right to the Appleby-Frodingham Co. and the Frodingham footbridge is plainly evident lower down.

Diagram from a contemporary issue of *The Railway Engineer* showing the extent of construction undertaken by the LNER in the late 1920s. the GCR 1918 yard proposals were located south of the then GCR station. The 'engine shed' is a misnomer - during the early days of the North Lindsey Light Railway contractor's locos were housed there. The site of the busy level crossing is easily discerned - the need for a road viaduct was obvious, and pressing.

ARRANGEMENT OF MAIN LINES AND SIDINGS BEFORE ALTERATIONS AND EXTENSIONS WERE CARRIED OUT.

ARRANGEMENT OF NEW MAIN LINES AND SIDINGS AT SCUNTHORPE AND FRODINGHAM, LONDON & NORT
Showing location of New Bridge carrying Ashby Road, New Station, Reinforced Concrete Footbridge and Viaduct, Goods Offices and Ware

panies were expected to contribute. In addition the government was in the process of deciding the structure of the country's railway system and it could be argued that the GCR would not spend money anyway, given its imminent demise. Boom conditions in the iron and steel trade continued until 1921, with 'traffic operating under difficulty and great risk'.

Interim work in progress. The up platform of Alexander Road station is virtually gone, while the down side buildings remain. The old route is being temporarily diverted to the new main line, up to the newly opened passenger station.

Matters were not still however, as the following extract from The Engineer of 30th March 1923 relates: 'Now that trade is returning to normal, the importance of improving the railway facilities at Scunthorpe & Frodingham is being urged. At present there is much congestion with poor, insufficient siding accommodation and most of the traffic passing through a 'bottleneck' before it reaches the main line. It is now authoritatively stated that Sir Berkeley Sheffield and Mr. R. Wedgwood, general manager of the LNER, were present at a recent meeting of the Lincolnshire Ironmasters Association in London. A plan is definitely agreed upon, to be done at once, to relieve congestion at the 'bottleneck'.

The further alterations, bridge over the road, new station, etc. will need Parliamentary powers and are under consideration. If these are agreed upon they will be included in the LNER Bill at the end of 1923.'

There was a never-ending problem at the 'bottleneck' and protracted, voluminous correspondence survives to record the settlement of the expanded layout at the eastern end of Trent Yard/Angle. The correspondence (along with the layout alterations themselves!) was prolonged over more than a decade through a three-sided

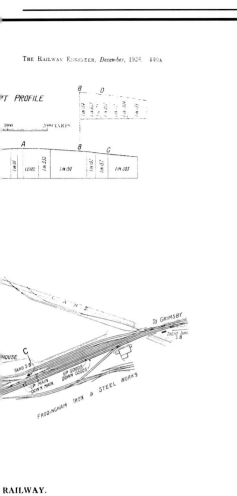

THE RAILWAY ENGINEER, *December*, 1928. 440A

Above. The spanking new LNER yard, 30th July 1929, looking west from the Brigg Road Viaduct. The old main line ran to the left of this yard, and the new line can be seen on the right. Yard No.1 signal box is visible with a 'Pom Pom' acting as travelling pilot. The Midland Ironstone branch bears off left, crossing Alexander Road. The houses behind, on Queen Street, were used by foreign train crews as lodgings between trips. Note the two electric light pylons illuminating the east end of the yard.

Below. Brigg Road Viaduct, though nowadays it would be termed a road bridge. Situated at the east end of New Yard, it was built in reinforced concrete, at a little over £66,000. The western curve to the North Lindsey Light Railway is in the foreground. The ground works and signalling do not seem to be in their final state by this date (12th May 1931); the chimneys of the original Frodingham steel melting shop stand out prominent on the right and the powerhouse boiler chimney, associated with the nearby blast furnaces, dominates the near skyline. The viaduct still stands though it has been rebuilt (1988) with consolidation at each end. The western curve connection has been filled in, thus isolating the western approach to the NLLR.

General view of the new goods yard, from the Brigg Road viaduct. The western curve to the North Lindsey Light Railway bears off northwards near the goods office (the neat, new brick building). The Trent Ironworks (soon to be closed) are in the distance looming behind the tranship shed. A yard hand appears to be having a breather, resting himself on the buffer stops.

The western end of the new Scunthorpe and Frodingham station, 30th July 1929, with engine smoke already coating the reinforced concrete footbridge. The new yard (west end) pilot (a J50 0-6-0T of the 1926 building programme) is working stock in the goods bay. Ashby Road Bridge is to the right and, on the far side of the train, stands the stationmaster's new house. The footbridge has since been rebuilt and is now covered. The goods bay is long out of use.

debate, between the Frodingham Ironstone Mines Co. (the Oswalds ironstone concern), the various iron and steel traders and the LNER.

The LNER authorities published a parliamentary bill in 1924; within it are the following relevant sections:-
'A Railway No.5 (1 mile 1 furlong 9.3 chains in length) in the Urban District of Scunthorpe & Frodingham commencing by a junction with the Company's Barnsley to Barnetby Railway west of Ashby Road and terminating by a junction with the said railway north east of Station Road Level Crossing.
'A Railway No. 6 (3 furlongs 6.65 chains in length) in the Urban District of

Scunthorpe & Frodingham commencing by a junction with Railway No.5 near Williamson Street and terminating by a junction with the Company's North Lindsey Light Railway near Dawes Lane Level Crossing.'

There was a section amongst the local merchants (as well as the proprietor of the Station Hotel) which objected to these long overdue proposals, on the grounds of insufficient financial compensation and depreciation of the property affected. In addition, the severing of the Brigg Road level crossing, being replaced by a road bridge over the proposed extensions, affected these merchants financially. But an important principle was at

stake, according to the legal department of the LNER, one which would have severely affected future railway bills. Consequently the bill was withdrawn during April 1924. According to the estate agent of Lord St. Oswald, the objections were 'an act of insanity after the years of agitation to get improved railway facilities. I hear (that) there is great dissatisfaction in Scunthorpe as you may imagine.' This gentleman, a Mr. Croft, referred to the '...old grievance of compensation when no land is taken.'

A little-recorded aspect of railway construction is 'land' but the correspondence and confrontation it caused was endless, even in the 1920s. Very soon after the bill's withdrawal, efforts were made to come to an agreement with the objectors, with the result that in the following July of 1925, the LNER gained an Act to proceed with land purchases and the rest of the legal niceties in order to lay down its extensions at Frodingham. Railways Nos 5 and 6 were replaced by the following:- 'A Railway No.4 (1 mile 1 furlong 9 chains in length) in the Urban District of Scunthorpe & Frodingham commencing by a junction ... 20.5 chains west of bridge and terminating by a junction ... 14.5 chains north east of Station Road Level Crossing.
'A Railway No. 5 (2 furlongs 6.5 chains in length) .. commencing by a junction ...3.5 chains north of line opposite north end of Queen Street otherwise Sixth Street North and terminating by a junction ... 5.75 chains south east of Dawes Lane Level Crossing'. This was not quite the same animal as that of 1924.
The principal landowner from whom the LNER bought this land for the New Yard and other works were the executors of the second Lord St. Oswald. Approximately 63 acres priced at roughly £47,000 changed hands, comprising buildings and farms, in other words, agricultural land - 65 separate properties, 14 separate transactions along with 27 individual occupiers were involved with the price of land varying from £1,210 to £300 per acre. This included any minerals underneath, and though the executors desired that minerals be paid for to be up to 1,000 ft below the surface, the LNER would not go beyond 200ft. This whole process entailed a mass of protracted correspondence, land maps and plans involving contentious points between the parties. Essentially, and in time-honoured fashion, it was one selling as high as possible, the other buying as cheap as possible. The position is best summarised by this LNER Report to the Traffic and Works Committee 26 Jan 1926:

FRODINGHAM AND SCUNTHORPE - PROPOSED IMPROVEMENTS
The question of effecting an improvement in the railway facilities at Frodingham

The new Frodingham footbridge, spanning the width of the new yard and main line, 30th July 1929. It was built in reinforced concrete and when a portion of the floor gave way in the mid-1950s the whole bridge was rebuilt. From the very beginnings of the railway a right of way existed from Scunthorpe Parish on the far side to Frodingham and Brumby Parishes and a footbridge existed from the first days. Since 1991 the yard has been closed and the whole scene will change at some future time. Coke wagons of the former Appleby Iron Co. along with ironstone hoppers of the Frodingham Iron & Steel Co. are in customary abundance. The latter were used on trains from the company's mines in South Lincolnshire.

has come before the Directors at various times since Amalgamation. It has been recognised that the Frodingham District has shown a remarkable development as an Iron and Steel producing Area, and that considerable further developments might reasonably be anticipated. It has further been generally recognised that the railway facilities in the Frodingham Area were in need of improvement in order to keep pace with the existing, and prospective developments. Finally, it has been recognised that the London & North Eastern Railway have at present the monopoly of the heavy and remunerative traffic to and from the Frodingham Works, and that this monopoly has for some time been jealously watched by our competitors whose system, by means of the Axholme Joint Railway, extends to within 10 miles of the Frodingham district, and who could, without excessive expense, invade the district and secure a large proportion of the traffic.

Aerial view, about 1958. The lines run across left from New Yard to Trent Junction on the right with Entrance 'E' (closed 1990) running south to the Appleby-Frodingham plant. The heavy section rolling mills fill the right hand side of the photograph. The 1920s Brigg Road viaduct and its diversion stands out as it crosses the railway with the former Station Road/Brigg Road route cut into two. A very busy level crossing formerly existed there. The North Lindsey Light and associated junctions are clearly shown, the light railway proceeding northwards out of frame. The enlarged LNER goods yard is in this triangle of lines with Frodingham shed between it and Dawes Lane. The white area alongside the shed is the spent chemical sludge from the water softener. Blast furnaces occupied the centre of picture until the mid-1950s; on the steelworks side of the railway opposite the shed and Trent up sidings, is Entrance 'D', also known as 'Cliff's' - the family name of the owners of the former Frodingham Iron Company.

The pristine new goods offices standing at the entrance to the new goods yard, in July 1929. This building is still standing. The weighbridge and the weighman's office stand opposite.

The road entrance to the new goods yard, which was completely remodelled and considerably enlarged by the LNER during the 1920s. The road itself was the original 'Station Road' in the town of Scunthorpe and led to the 1883 station, across a very busy and often dangerous level crossing. The new goods offices are on the left, the new goods warehouse at the end of the road - behind that is the power house boiler chimney of the Frodingham Iron & Steel Works blast furnaces. Crossing in the foreground are the lines of the western curve, connecting the North Lindsey Light Railway with the main through lines at Yard No.1.

the 5th October, 1923 the Board sanctioned he inclusion of these proposals in the Company's Bill for 1924. Owing to certain opposition on the part of Local Property Owners this item in the Bill was, however, abandoned until a later date.

3. The same scheme was included in the Powers sought under the Company's Bill for 1925, sanction being given under Board Minute 371. These Powers were duly obtained and the Bill became Law on the 31st July, 1925; since that date the scheme has been receiving the detailed consideration of the Company's Officers, and the proposals are now ready for submission in detail, to the Committee.

The general case for the expenditure is well known to the Committees; some more detailed figures may, however, be helpful. The general volume of traffic at Frodingham (including Normanby Park) has advanced to a maximum in the year 1923. From that date, in sympathy with the general depression in the Iron and Steel Trade, it has declined but it still stands at a figure considerably in excess of the maximum reached in the year 1913. The annual tonnages of goods, coal and coke traffic for the year 1913 and onwards have been as follows:-

Year	Tons
1913	3,248,032
1914	2,996,071
1915	3,157,356
1916	3,468,453
1917	3,678,022
1918	3,627,637
1919	3,239.990
1920	3,979,958
1921	1,185,975
1922	2,823,005
1923	4,433,802
1924	4,194,247
1925	3,730,652

The present depression may be taken as being of a temporary character only. Even if the Iron & Steel Trade should not succeed in reaching the pre-war level of prosperity it may be taken that the Frodingham district, having regard to the many advantages which it possesses in cheap raw material, is likely to benefit more markedly than the older Steel producing Areas from any recovery in the Iron & Steel Trade as a whole. It is at present working very far below its full capacity, and without additional capital expenditure is in a position to avail itself very rapidly of any improvement in the Market.

The number of Blast Furnaces is 23 of which 12 only are in blast at the present time.

The Appleby Iron Company contemplate proceeding immediately with the construction of their new Steel Works, the output from which is expected to be about 200,000 tons of Steel plates per annum. In connection with the manufacture of this

On all these grounds it has been felt that the district is one which should receive special consideration in the matter of railway facilities. Unfortunately, up to the present moment, owing to a variety of considerations, it has not been possible to put forward any very satisfactory scheme of improvement, and the district has undoubtedly been sufferin, rather severely from inadequate railway accommodation. The position has been receiving continuous attention since the formation of the Amalgamated Company.

1. On the 8th June, 1923, the Board sanctioned the provision of additional sidings at Frodingham at a cost of £37,940. The Traders undertook certain Works estimated to cost £35,000 in continuation of the Sidings, and the money spent on both sides has undoubtedly been of great assistance since the work was completed in April, 1925. At the same time this extension was put forward merely as a temporary measure and was so regarded when sanctioned by the Board.

2. A larger scheme for improvements at Frodingham was receiving consideration at this time, and under their Minute of

The new goods tranship shed on 30th July 1929. This was one of the LNER extensions to the goods yard which, even before the Great War, was very cramped. A variety of road wagons, lorries and a distinctive motorcar add interest to a splendid period scene. Small goods were collected and delivered locally and transhipped to other similar centres in full wagon loads. Now flattened, the blast furnaces of the Frodingham Works are across the line behind. The car with the 'Dickey' seat appears to be a 'Star' or a 'Bean' model.

quantity of steel it is estimated that about 800,000 tons per annum of iron ore, coal and other materials would require to be carried by rail to Frodingham.

It is anticipated that the whole of the Works at Frodingham, including the extensions which have been carried out, will be in full working order by the Summer, and recent increases which have taken place in the traffic afford ground for a hopeful view of the situation.

Our Officers responsible for the operation of the traffic report that very serious difficulty is encountered in handling the existing volume of business, and should there be any moderate revival in traffic very serious congestion and delays would occur. The Manufacturers and representatives of the district have, on the whole, shown great patience with the railway difficulties which they have experienced

Apart from the 'Scunthorpe' station on the North Lindsey Light there were three stations of that name on the main line - this is the third and last, 'Scunthorpe & Frodingham'. The photograph was taken during 1934 from the grounds of the stationmaster's new residence. The station building is little altered externally to this day - a no frills, mid-1920s approach to station architecture.

1929, and an almost rural scene compared with today. Scunthorpe & Frodingham station box stands at the end of the down (Doncaster) platform with the approach lines to the new yard across the foreground. The fine new residence beyond the box and the other side of the main line is the stationmaster's house. It was said to be very draughty and hard to keep warm even with plentiful (free) coal. The houses on the right were also substantial, belonging to steelworks gaffers - now all are solicitors' offices and so on. A hotel now occupies the land behind the stationmaster's house, which was later demolished to make way for a car park.

in the past, but it is to be feared that if there should be a serious repetition of the inconveniences which they experienced in 1923 and in preceding years, there would be a concerted move made to get the London Midland & Scottish into the district.

The numbers of wagons - loaded and empty - to and from Frodingham during the year 1924 were 363,944 received and 364,649 forwarded; the North Lindsey Light Railway received 123,610 and forwarded 121,562. In the 6 months ended June 30th 1925 figures were 169,852 received and 169,266 forwarded at Frodingham and 60,721 and 60,744 respectively on the North Lindsey Light Railway.

During the year 1924, the number of wagons in and out averaged 3,121 per day. The proposals now put forward provide for:-

Estimated Cost

(i)	A new Passenger Station	£25,705
(ii)	A new marshalling yard, diversion of the main lines, and provision of up and down goods lines.	£168,206
(iii)	An enlarged goods and coal yard with new warehouse and new Goods Office	£37,170
(iv)	Diversion of road, with new bridge over railway to enable the level crossing east of the present passenger station to be abolished	£68,000
(v)	A western curve between the main	

lines and the North Lindsey Light Railway	£8,692
Total estimated cost of new works	£307,773
Expenditure on land already authorised	£23,559
Estimate cost of land still be acquired	£9,000
TOTAL	£340,332

The several parts of the scheme are dealt with in greater detail below:-

(i) NEW PASSENGER STATION Estimated cost £25,705
The scheme of improvements necessitates the removal of the passenger station to a new site a short distance to the west, and as the town is developing in the westerly direction, the altered position will be more convenient for the residential population. It is proposed to provide such accommodation and facilities as will adequately meet the requirements of the district. The population of Frodingham and Scunthorpe has increased from 19,360 in 1911 to 27,354 in 1921, or over 40 per cent. It will not be necessary for any additional staff to be employed at the new station.

(ii) MARSHALLING YARD - Estimated Cost £168,206
For many years, great difficulty has been experienced in dealing with the heavy traffic to and from Frodingham. The present marshalling sidings provide accommodation for 2,205 wagons. There are no reception sidings and the trains have

to stop on the main running lines to detach wagons for the various works and sidings. This results in great delay to trains detaching and holds up other trains in the rear.
It is, therefore, proposed to provide a separate marshalling yard, with reception sidings, to enable trains from the west to be dealt with clear of the main lines immediately on arrival so that the engines may be liberated. The wagons will then be sorted and worked forward to the various works by pilot engines. The train delays which now occur will be materially reduced and it will be unnecessary - as is frequently the case at the present time - to hold back at other places traffic which is required by the firms but which cannot be accepted at Frodingham owing to the absence of facilities for dealing with it.
The accommodation which it is proposed to provide in the new yard consists of:-

	Capacity
2 reception roads	166 wagons
20 sorting sidings	1,716 wagons
TOTAL	1,882 wagons

with the necessary shunting spurs. Provision is also made for three short sidings which will hold 78 crippled wagons.
The new yard will be mainly used for traffic FROM the west destined for the various works at Frodingham and for the North Lindsey Light Railway, but traffic

TO the west from the North Lindsey Light Railway which cannot be worked on through trains and traffic from the Midland Ironstone Company will also be dealt with in the yard.

Traffic from the east for the Frodingham Firms will be detached into the various works direct from down trains as at present, but wagons for the North Lindsey Light Railway will be taken into the new yard and placed with others from the west to be worked to destination on the booked trains.

The existing sidings at Frodingham will be almost exclusively used for marshalling OUTWARDS traffic for destination points both east and west.

The provision of up and down goods lines from a point on the west side of the new passenger station would obviate a good deal of the delay which now takes place to trains to and from Grimsby and Immingham owing to their being held up by trains having work to perform at Frodingham, as with the additional facilities, they could be given a clear run through that place.

It is estimated that 15 additional men would be required to work the new yard, and that their wages would amount to £2,644 per annum.

At the present time, 5 pilot engines are employed at Frodingham for an aggregate of 104 engine hours per day. The new yard would necessitate the provision of an additional engine and an increase in engine hours of 24 per day, involving an expenditure of £3,806 per annum.

The estimated additional cost for staff and pilot engine power is, therefore, £6,450 per annum.

On the other hand, the new yard would enable a considerable reduction in train delays to be effected:-

(a) On the basis of records taken during weeks ended July 11th and November 7th, 1925, the delays to trains approaching Frodingham in both directions amount to 14,612 hours per annum, representing a loss of £10,959. It is estimated that at least 75% of these delays would be obviated and an annual saving effected of £8,219.

(b) At the present time, wagons for the various Works at Frodingham are marshalled in the trains at the points where they are attached and considerable delay is thereby caused to these trains and others in the rear. The wagons would be taken unmarshalled to the new yard and it is estimated that the annual savings in engine time which could be effected at various places would amount to £2,137.

(c) A number of trains which are at present booked to terminate at Frodingham detach wagons at the various works and sidings. Under the proposed scheme, these trains would dispose of their wagons in the new yard, and it is estimated that, in the aggregate, a reduction in train engine time of 3,094 hours per annum could be brought about representing a saving of £2,320.

(d) An average of about 18 engines per day are turned on the triangle at the east end of Frodingham one side of which is the property of the Appleby Iron Company, and considerable delay takes place in turning owing to the occupation of the lines. Under the proposed scheme, these engines, on being released from their trains at the new yard, would be turned on the triangle which would be formed by the western curve to the North Lindsey Light Railway, and it is estimated that a saving of 20 minutes per engine would be effected. This would mean a reduction of 1,872 engine hours, representing an annual saving of £1,404

The total annual saving under the foregoing heads is, therefore, £14,080.

The additional accommodation for 594 wagons, which was authorised in June 1923 and completed in April 1925, has effected a considerable reduction in the delays to trains at and approaching Frodingham. The delays during week ended May 13th, 1923 - before the accommodation was provided - amounted to 588 hours compared with 255 hours during week ended July 11th, 1925, and 307 hours during week ended November 7th, 1925.

The central portion of the station frontage, showing in some detail the stonework framing the tall windows and the dominant sides to the entrance. The canopy over the entrance way, with 'Scunthorpe and Frodingham' cut out, is long gone, possibly in the wartime scrap drive.

A mishap adjacent to Yard No.1 signal box, at the east end of New Yard. The date is unknown but as the nameboards have gone, the guess is World War Two or shortly thereafter. It might be that a trip working has become derailed entering New Yard from the east - witness the brakevan on its side - or maybe (given the piled up wagon stock) there has been a runaway, out of one of the sidings in New Yard. Any offers? Photograph G. Askew Collection.

(iii) ENLARGED GOODS AND COAL YARD WITH NEW WAREHOUSE - Estimated Cost £37,170

The accommodation in the present Goods Yard is inadequate for the traffic which has to be dealt with, the wagon capacity being:-

Goods traffic - 141 wagons
Coal traffic - 22 wagons
Total 163 wagons

The number of LOADED wagons dealt with in the goods yard during week ended December 19th, 1925 was 398 received and 251 forwarded, an average of over a hundred a day. The average number of coal wagons standing under load each day during the week was 104.

It is proposed to enlarge the yard and increase the accommodation to hold:-

Goods Traffic - 258 wagons
Coal Traffic - 55 wagons
Total 313 wagons.

The present goods warehouse - which holds only 4 wagons - has become too small for the requirements. The proposed new warehouse will accommodate 10 wagons. The average daily tonnage dealt with in the present warehouse in 9.5 tons, while the traffic which is handled daily in the open, but which ought to be dealt with under cover, is 37.5 tons.

Some of the goods clerical staff are at present accommodated in the original station buildings, which are separated from the main goods office. The proposed alterations will necessitate the removal of the old buildings and the scheme provides for a new office to accommodate 33 clerks near the entrance to the yard. The concentration of the clerks in one office will obviate the waste of time which now takes place by the staff having to walk to and fro in connection with their work.

(iv) DIVERSION OF ROAD WITH NEW BRIDGE OVER RAILWAY - Estimated Cost £68,000

At the present time there are only two lines - one up and one down - through Frodingham and the position is complicated by the existence of an important public road level crossing adjacent to the present passenger station. The railway and road traffic passing over this level crossing is considerable and it is of the utmost importance that, in the interests alike of the railway and road traffic, it should be abolished. Powers have been obtained to close the crossing and a portion of the roadway leading to it, subject to the construction by the Company of a new road which will cross the railway by an overbridge. This will enable the goods yard to be enlarged and extended over the site of the existing public road and onto the land west thereof.

(v) WESTERN CURVE TO THE NORTH LINDSEY LIGHT RAILWAY - Estimated Cost £8,692

The provision of the Western Curve would enable through trains to be run direct from points west of Frodingham and from the new marshalling yard to the North Lindsey Light Railway and vice versa. This would obviate the necessity of the traffic being passed over the busy lines and sidings east of the present passenger station and along the Eastern Curve.

It is proposed to work over the Western Curve each day 12 trains to and 8 trains from the Light Railway, the bulk of the traffic being to and from Messrs. Lysaght's Works at Normanby Park.

Based on present traffic, it would be possible to run two through trains each way daily between Wath and Ardsley respectively and Normanby Park and Yorkshire Mines, while the traffic which does not pass in sufficient quantities to enable through trains to be made up from or to any particular point would be passed through the new marshalling yard, pilot trips being run to and from the Light Railway. Certain trains for the west with outwards traffic from the Light Railway would start from the new yard instead of from the Eastern sidings as at present.

It is estimated that the saving in train mileage by working traffic to and from the Light Railway by means of the proposed curve instead of through the sidings to the east of Frodingham would amount to 3,153 miles per annum, which would effect a saving of £509.

Traffic from the Light Railway for destinations East of Frodingham would, as far as possible, continue to be conveyed via the Eastern Curve.

Little appears to have altered by 1964, other than the appearance of the British Railways blue enamelled nameboard.

(vi) ENGINE SHED

It will be observed from the plan that a site is allocated for a new engine shed on land which has been acquired for this purpose. It is roughly estimated that the expenditure which would be involved in the provision of locomotive facilities would be in the neighbourhood of £300,000 which it is felt could not be justified at the present time, and it will be necessary for this part of the scheme to undergo further examination. Meanwhile, it is considered that this should not delay the carrying out of the other improvements.

SUMMARY OF ESTIMATES
Cost of Scheme -   £340,332

ADDITIONAL ANNUAL CHARGES
Staff -   £2,644
Locomotive Power -   £3,806
Maintenance -   £3,592

TOTAL   £10,042

SAVINGS
Engine Time -   £14,080
Train mileage -   £509
TOTAL   £14,589

It is, therefore, RECOMMENDED that authority be given for the expenditure of £307,773.

Signed etc.
26th January 1926.

****

A few comments would not be out of place in order to flesh out the above Memorandum. History was in the minds of the LNER hierarchy - hence reference to the LMSR 'invading' the district. Soon after the formation of the North Lindsey Light the Lancashire & Yorkshire Railway had seen the possibilities of storming the GCR monopoly - hence the construction of the Axholme Joint Railway on the other side of the River Trent. LYR designs upon the Frodingham ironstone field rested on gaining control of the North Lindsey Light and the mechanism would have been by share purchase from an eager-to-sell coterie of NLLR Directors. However, the GCR stepped in during 1906/07 and secured the controlling interest. The LYR (and NER) operated the Axholme Joint and the infant LMS may have resurrected the proposed invasion. The Frodingham ironstone, pig iron, steel and coal traffic was very lucrative indeed but as far as can be gathered the LMSR had no real expansionist intent.

The introduction to the Memorandum makes the point that no satisfactory

Cold comfort indeed! The interior of the waiting room on the Doncaster platform in 1964. No coal fire, only the utility electric heater that cut out after a few minutes. The original benches and fireplace remain but now the room is more customer-friendly, with adverts.

No indication of an 'open station' in 1964; the ticket barrier and inspection cabin at Scunthorpe - 2/9d for a return to Doncaster was the commencement of a day's treat for many a local lad. The lack-lustre notices of this period are displayed along with a selection of 'dailies' on the table.

1925. A further 'guessestimate' suggests that each train was, on average, half an hour late - an extraordinary cost over a year. One can readily appreciate the problems, for a look at the working timetables reveal that upwards of 200 trains were booked into and out of Frodingham per weekday - apart from the additional numerous special and relief trains, often put on at short notice.

Local sources of information concerning the construction of the LNER extensions are scarce (the only local newspaper of the time was a weekly and that was based at Brigg some miles away). However, an account of these improvements was given in The Railway Engineer for December 1928 by which time the job was virtually complete.

A total of 200,000 cubic yards of excavation was dealt with, in two operations. The spoil for the new yard and main lines was removed first, and the main lines laid in their altered position, so that the remaining earth (under the old main lines) could be removed. This material was tipped to form the new approaches to the road viaduct as well as to level up the site for the new goods yard.

Three separate contracts were let. The lengthening and widening of the Ashby Road bridge, at the western end of the New Works, went to Fletcher & Co. of Mansfield. This bridge carried the main Scunthorpe to Gainsborough road and was begun first as it formed the accesss to the new yard. The National Strike made for a shortage of structural steel (here of all places!) and delays ensued but, with the new span already in place the old bridge was blown up and demolished on Sunday 17th July 1927.

The second contract (to Caffin & Co. Ltd. of London) was for the provision of new sidings, the new alignment of the

scheme had been put forward 'owing to the variety of considerations'. Whether this was due to local circumstances already referred to or that the LNER was short of money, or both, is not clear. However, work soon commenced upon construction of these extensions once the various LNER committees gave the nod.

Further into the account mention is made of only 12 out of 23 local blast furnaces in actual operation ('in blast'). The LNER was quite optimistic as regards future prospects for the local iron and steel trade; output did pick up after the National Strike of 1926 but crashed soon after in 1929, with the onset of the Great Slump. It was not until 1934 that production accelerated. Frodingham, though, did not suffer anywhere near as much as other industrial centres during these economic doldrums. The one great advantage of Frodingham was the production of very cheap iron and this fact carried through into the production of steel. Not that there was no hardship - Redbourn steel-making capacity lay dormant for quite a while, and traffic levels were generally low.

The details given of wagons received and forwarded locally for 1924 and the first half of 1925 indicate the scale of the whole enterprise. Throughout this period approximately 3,000 wagons per day were moving into and out of the Frodingham complex. Even a conservative 'guessestimate' yields the equivalent of a goods/mineral train every 20 minutes or so throughout the working day (assum-

ing 312 working days per year) and this scale of operation remained until dieselisation much later. There was a lot of overtime collected by crews, hanging about with their engines in sidings and loops on the Frodingham approaches and it is easy to appreciate the low priority given to local passenger traffic.

Another aspect of local conditions comes later, when reference is made to delays to trains for two weekly periods in

Pedal power at Scunthorpe & Frodingham station in 1964, deposited by the local commuters in somewhat random fashion on the Cleethorpes platform. The mail van is visible in the up bay, with a trolley load of papers and magazines ready to be delivered to the town's shops. Most of the Scunthorpe workers used bikes but the thrice daily shift change is all but a memory nowadays - it's all private cars with taxis.

main lines, closing of the level crossing adjoining the old station, construction of a new road and viaduct to replace this latter crossing and a new footbridge to span the new yard and running lines. The original footbridge over the old main line carried a public footpath between the parishes of Frodingham and Brumby to the south and Scunthorpe to the north. The new bridge was much longer than the lattice girder original, 371ft long in reinforced concrete. The excavation was started during December 1926, the contractor using a Ruston 20 ton steam navvy. The length of the road viaduct was 400ft, at 15ft above rail level with a 30ft road running over. This new road viaduct and approaches were opened for traffic in June 1928.

The third contract was let for construction of the new station, three quarters of a mile west of the old one, the partial demolition of the old structure and construction of a new goods yard, warehouse and goods offices. The new station had platforms 600ft long with a bay platform and cattle dock at the east end and a loading dock at the west end. It was opened on a cold, snowy Sunday, 11th March 1928. Again the contractor was Caffin & Co.

About 18 miles of track were laid in the new sidings with a capacity for 1,700 wagons along with a further 160 in the new goods yard. All the permanent way work was carried out by the LNER's District Engineer. The design of the new works was undertaken by C.J. Brown, the Chief Engineer (Southern Area) and his team. Local supervision was by R.F. Bennett, the Assistant Engineer for Construction.

Above. The ticket window and occupant in 1964. There have been no alterations since building by the LNER nearly forty years earlier. The mandatory 'Conditions of Carriage' notice is prominently displayed along with the passenger timetable. Austere in the extreme to modern eyes but, in its day, the place was admired for its pre-Second World War standard of detail.

Below. The hidden interior. Everything written down, stamped and logged. Now long swept away, the system was a wonder of tickets, of every hue and type. Pre-decimal coinage at the ready for change, even the scissors have their place.

Above. Frodingham engine shed, viewed from the south west, six months prior to opening. The structure is up and the shed is being fitted out.

Below. Interior of the shed 31st December 1931. A great deal of inside work requires to be done. Note the smoke vents running the full length of the structure. The girder supports are stamped 'Sands, Colwick, Notts, British Steel'. The contractor was a Nottingham firm and the British steel industry was in the depths of recession, with steel imports adding to the woe.

Chapter Five

FRODINGHAM ENGINE SHED

As we have seen, from Great Central times on there was acute aware ness of the need for an engine shed at Frodingham - how could it not be, given the conditions at Keadby? and in fact, serious proposals as to the purchase of a site had been proceeded with. But the endemic local problem, that of finding a suitable site relatively cheaply priced, without ironstone lying underneath the surface, could not be overcome. Even the LNER, in its *Memo* of the previous chapter, put off the evil hour.

The greater part of goods services to and from Frodingham were, perforce, worked by engines and crews from other sheds though Keadby, as we have seen, provided the base for the local pilot and shunting engines along with engines for some goods trains. Coal and other services from the west were powered by Mexborough engines and crews and Grimsby (later Immingham) shed performed a similar function to the east. Most jobs were easily encompassed within the 12 hour, later 10 hour shift but the 8 hour day, gained by railwaymen during 1919,

dramatically changed the situation. A considerable number of extra men were taken on at Keadby to cover the local goods operations - the working day had been reduced, in theory, by 20% and substantial changes were inevitable. Mexborough and Immingham crews continued to work into the area but the large expansion in iron and steel production demanded more local engines.

Keadby of course was wholly unsatisfactory with regard to facilities, amenities and location (as described earlier) and with the uncertainty as to the outcome of the national railway system after the Great War, the GCR (again as we have seen) was unlikely to spend money on a new shed at Frodingham. Like the new yard and other improvements, it was up to the LNER to 'foot the bill', as Chapter Four describes.

The land for the engine shed, the site of the former Lindsey Iron Works adjoining Dawes Lane, was purchased at the same time as that for the yard extensions though the approximate figure of £300,000 estimated for the shed and its facilities

does not even roughly square up to the cost when finally built - about £105,000 in 1932, the year the shed opened for use. The site accounted for a similar sum. It is suggested that a much grander establishment was initially envisaged but no details are known. The final cost was less than half that of the 1926 estimate but it was still a relatively expensive proposition, as the entire edifice had to be built well *above* the ground surface, in order to match the levels of the surrounding railway lines. This made for vaulting, cathedral-like foundations reaching down many feet, for the shed, turntable, engine and ash pits, and it was as well that Government financial assistance was available for such projects. Soon after the new yard extensions had opened, traffic volumes decreased sharply with the Depression and it was not until the grant provisions of the 1929 Loans and Guarantees Act were available for national railway works that the LNER could proceed with the work. An LNER Traffic Committee minute of 20th March 1930 had estimated the work at £104,220, with 'the capital pro-

Frodingham shed soon after opening during August 1932. The five road reinforced concrete shed was home for 51 engines, though this was the depths of depression. A 'Tiny' 0-8-0 is having attention to its smokebox over one of the pits while an O4 and one or two other engines lurk inside. The offices, shops and messrooms were alongside the southern shed wall, with the clerk's office at the west end. Doors were fitted but were soon wrecked; it made for a very draughty situation but a vast improvement on the Keadby site. By the 1950s the allocation was approximately 70 engines.

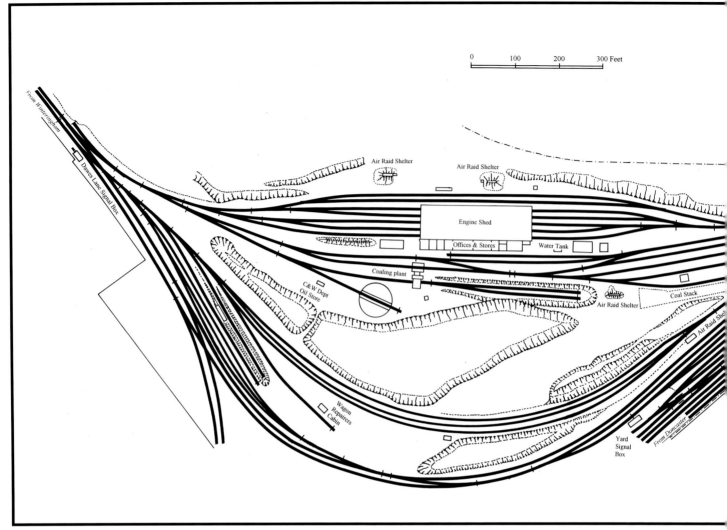

portion on which the government grant was based' being £102,970.

The contract forms for the construction of the 'New Locomotive Depot at Frodingham, Engine Shed and Other Works' were issued in October 1930 under the name of Charles J. Brown, the Chief Engineer of the LNER. The tender submitted by G.A. Pillatt & Son, of Nottingham on 20th October was accepted by the LNER on the 25th of the same month, the quote being £32,705.7s.8d, no less (astonishing how accurate one could be in those days). Twelve months was the length of time given to complete the job. 'The Works' included 'construction of a reinforced concrete engine shed, the substructure for a 50,000 gallon tank, the foundations for a 70ft engine turntable, water columns, coal hoist, wheel drop and other works all as represented upon the Plans and Drawings ...'

Breaking down this sum into the component parts gave the following:-

General conditions	£870
Reinforced concrete engine shed	£16259.17s.7d
Substructure for 50,000 gallon tank	£1771.12s.8d
Engine pits	£9247.1s.6d
Foundations for 70ft engine turntable	£1393.15s.10d
Foundations for water columns and coal hoist	£457.12s.9d
Foundations for wheel drop	£841.9s.0d
Sundry items	£1714.18s.4d
Maintenance of Works	£125

A Frodingham 'Daisy', No.69905, on shed during April 1956. It was one of the LNER-built batch initially fitted with a booster (note cut down side tanks). By the time they arrived at Frodingham the engines were run down and not much suitable work could be found. Photograph A.R. Goult/D. Jackson Collection.

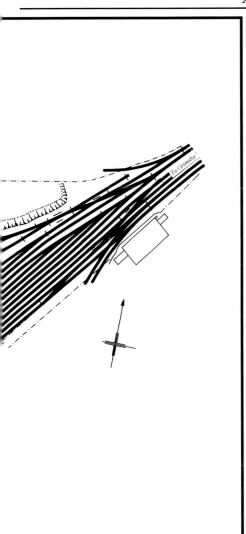

Former GCR 8A 'Tiny', Q4 No.63236 at the rear of Frodingham shed, 11th March 1951. Photograph J. Oxley.

This locomotive shed was aligned (perhaps unfortunately) east-west and was originally fitted with 16ft high by 14ft wide galvanised steel revolving shutters at each end, on each through road - luxurious for an engine shed at the time. The cost came to £772.4s.8d but in practical terms the doors soon became a hindrance. With constant use, a corrosive local atmosphere and frequent 'knocks' from engines, they were soon disposed of, though no date for their removal has been ascertained. Other features to suffer after a relatively short time were the smoke vents on the roof above the engine roads. They were of poor design, in concrete - a material with which there was relatively little experience at the time, at least in this sort of application.

The 'fixtures and fittings' for the new shed were obtained under separate headings. The coal hoist, of the elevated bucket type, was erected by W.W. Jenkins & Co. of Retford at a cost of £602.6s.6d., Messrs. Ransomes & Rapier won the work for the wheel drop and turntable, at a cost of £1,015. The hot water boiler washing plant was priced at £1,825 and the order was gained by the Economical Boiler Washing Co., a firm enjoying a number of LNER shed contracts during these years.

The water columns were supplied by J. Blakeborough & Sons of Woodhouse Works, Brighouse in Yorkshire at a cost of £217.10s.0d each. Cowans & Sheldon supplied the water cranes at a cost of £71.5s each.

The shed was designed to accommodate twenty engines under cover. There were fourteen examination and preparation pits each 50ft long, and the ash pits were 200ft long with an ash wagon road between. A small fitting and machine shop as well as a repair shop was provided, with second-hand machinery, transferred from other locomotive sheds in the Southern Area of the LNER. Further facilities included a small sand drier, five WCs, offices, stores, messrooms, electrical lighting, signalling and telephones. In fact, some of the mechanical equipment was brought up from Keadby shed, items valued, with some optimism, at £400. Eight locomotives were transferred from Immingham in order to cut down on light engine and train crew travelling costs from there - with the engines transferred from Keadby this brought the Frodingham allocation to 45 upon opening in June 1932.

Two additional features were yet to be laid down at the shed. One year after opening the Locomotive Committee ap-

Looking a bit care-worn, on 11th March 1951, is Frodingham L3 69051. The engines were used as tripping pilots between the yards at Frodingham. Photograph J. Oxley.

£6,500. The existing plant transferred was later to Hitchin shed. Apart from expediting the coaling of engines the scheme enabled seven men 'to be dispensed with'. Within three years the number of engines at Frodingham had increased from 45 to 51, comprising class 04, Q4, J11, J50, L1, a Y3 Sentinel and an ex-GNR D2.

The extensive foundation work meant that the turntable was not ready for the shed's opening and for a short period locomotives turned at the western/eastern curve leading from the main line on to the North Lindsey Light Railway. Prior to this, two options were available. One was a relatively precarious short journey around the triangular layout at the North Lincoln end of Trent Yard, where a side of the layout was a private railway belonging to the Appleby Iron Co. This often entailed running between and adjacent to ladles of molten pig iron proceeding from these works to Appleby Steel Melting Shop; some considerable caution was necessary and the transit had to be paid for. The second option was the triangle of junctions between Brocklesby, Ulceby and Habrough station, as well as the turntable at Wrawby Junction, Barnetby. This however entailed considerable extra mileage - altogether a 25 mile or so round trip, and men's wages on top.

After the Second World War, the local engine complement increased considerably, until at its peak some 60/70 were at Frodingham. This often caused congestion and with engines arriving/departing on steel, mineral and empty wagon trains, much inducement, often financial in the form of a guaranteed 12 hours, was given in order to clear the shed and keep traffic moving. For a trainspotter it was a sheer delight!

Frodingham Locomotive Shed c.1958

There were 141 sets of footplatemen and 4 cleaners.
68 locomotives: 5 J11 0-6-0s; 5 J50 0-6-0Ts, 28 04 2-8-0s, 21 WD 2-8-0s, 7 Q1 0-8-0Ts and 2 S1 0-8-4Ts. All received repairs up to the 'heavy' category. Examinations every 3-5 weeks, then 7-9 weeks and then every 5,000; 10,000; 15,000; 20,000; 25,000 and 30,000 miles. A boiler examination was undertaken every 6 months by a boiler inspector. A mechanical foreman performed a general examination on the locomotives every 12 months and a main works visit was made after about 60,000 miles, which occurred after about two and a half years. The goods locomotives averaged 1,800 - 2,000 miles per month.

Extracts from Frodingham Local Departmental Committee

10th January 1934
Appendix 'A' to minute no. 24,
Frodingham weekly list; Link working:-

The newly-erected water softening plant at the east end of Frodingham shed, 1934. Before the shed opened there was only a single water column available, built close to the North Lindsey Light Railway in 1912 and supplied from the town mains. The LNER tapped into a pipeline which had originally fed the closed North Lincolnshire Iron Works, the water originating from artesian boreholes near Appleby station. The LNER instigated a programme of softening locomotive feed water at many locations south of York from the early 1930s and the arrangements made with the North Lincolnshire Iron Co. (for the whole of the water at Frodingham, including the new shed) envisaged some 36 million gallons per year, at 1/- per 1000 gallons. The water was very hard; the softening plant had a capacity of 6,250 gallons per hour and, fortuitously, a 'natural pit' adjoined the shed, convenient for the waste sludge.

proved a report from the Chief Mechanical Engineer, Nigel Gresley, and the Divisional General Manager, Southern Area, recommending a water softening plant. The local water was, and is, notoriously hard and with engine boilers suffering from persistent and frequent scaling it was deemed essential that a softening plant be erected. The supply itself came from a borehole two miles west of the shed (near Appleby station); it supplied one of the steel works and the LNER, on the appropriate payment, tapped into it. It even obtained the electricity (to pump the water) from another local works. Total annual water consumption at this time was

of the order of 60 million gallons. The plant itself was a standard lime softening version from United Water Softeners Ltd., costing £1,300.

On 6th November 1936, the same Locomotive Committee discussed the provision of a bunker-type coaling plant for Frodingham. When the shed was opened in June 1932 coal consumed was about 370 tons per week but by 1936 this had risen to about 700 tons. This was due to the growth in traffic and with large quantities of coal the bucket plant was proving uneconomical. The proposal was for a skip-fed bunker type coaling plant of 100 tons capacity and the estimated cost was

No.1 Link - Banking Pilot
No.2 Link - Train Jobs
No.3 Link - Train Jobs
No.4 Link - Train Jobs
No.5 Link - Normanby Park Pilot
No.6 Link - Pilots
No.7 Link - Keadby No.3 Pilot (Sentinel)
Drivers to be booked in seniority order in the link - counting No.1 as the senior link. Firemen to be booked in seniority order in the links as follows: Senior men - No.1 Link and in seniority order in the following links:- No.5 Link, No.6 Link, No.2 Link, No.3 Link, No.4 Link

27th September 1938

Minute No.98 - Banking of trains between Gunhouse Junction and Frodingham: Keadby No.2 Banking Pilot - the Company's representatives stated they agreed to the banking of trains between Gunhouse Junction and Frodingham being performed tender first for a trial period of 3 months and the question to be reviewed at the end of that period.

4th October 1939

No.138 - Application for the provision of lockers, Enginemen's Mess Room - the Company's representatives stated that the application could not be conceded.
1st February 1945
Appendix 'A' to minute No.201
Seniority of Links shall be as follows:-

Link No	Name of Link
1	1st Gds / Coal Link
2	2nd Passenger, Goods and Coal Link
3	3rd Goods / Coal Link
4	Relief Link
5	1st Pilot Link
6	2nd Pilot Link
7	3rd Pilot Link
8	4th Pilot Link
9	5th Pilot Link
10	6th Pilot Link
11	7th Pilot Link
12	8th Pilot Link

Firemen will work through the links in seniority order in the following order:- No.12, No.11, No.10, No.9, No.3, No.2, No.1, No.4 (if any vacancies), ditto No.7, No.5, No.6 and No.8.

14th January 1948

No. 288 - Employees side; request to discuss the question of the shortage of Footplate Staff at Frodingham Depot - the Employee's Side stated that the shortage of Footplate Staff was preventing men from obtaining higher grade turns and retarding the work at the Depot. The Employer's Side gave details of the present position for staff and the arrangements for obtaining new entrants to the service.
(a) The Employee's Side suggested that more L3 class engines should be allocated to the depot to avoid tender first working which, they stated, had caused men to leave the service. The Employer's Side stated they would endeavour to obtain

Termed locally 'The Cenotaph' - the mechanical coaling tower, built during 1938. A simple steel framed hoist had been put up in 1932 for about 370 tons of coal per week but by November 1937 it was reported to the Locomotive Committee that consumption had risen to 700 tons per week, as traffic recovered from the Great Slump. The replacement was this bunker type plant of 100 tons capacity, costing approximately £6,500. The nearby Appleby-Frodingham Iron & Steel Co. supplied the requisite electrical power at 1d per unit which Gresley considered reasonable. Seven men were dispensed with on the introduction of this bunker plant. The engine turntable is in the foreground with the photographer's tripod mounted in the wagon.

more engines of this class for allocation to Frodingham.
(b) Medical examination re-arrangements.
(c) Loan of passed cleaners from Doncaster to Frodingham.
(d) Lack of advertising of railway jobs.
(e) Deferment for military service.
(f) Staff to co-operate with lodgings.
(g) Advertisements on company's stations and parcel vans.

10th February 1949

No.316 - Employee's Side - Complaint respecting alleged bad condition of footboards on tank engines - it was stated that the design of the footboards on Q1 class

engines makes its difficult to keep them in good condition. The Employer's Side agreed to make suitable alterations to overcome the difficulty.
No.317 - Employee's Side - Complaint respecting alleged bad condition of the front ends of tank engines. The Employee's Side suggested that the condition of the front ends of tank engines would keep in better condition by rearranging the system of changing pilots on the various jobs requiring a different class of engine. The Employer's Side agreed to try as an experiment an arrangement whereby the same class of engine was provided at the changeover of the pilots.

18th March 1952
No.459 - Staff Side; Frodingham No.10 Pilot; Complaint respecting loading - the Management Side stated it is considered that a run of wagons to 80 is a reasonable one and the instructions to this effect have been renewed. The Staff Side stated they do not agree with the views of the Management Side.

8th April 1954
No.533 - Staff Side to raise the question of certain Austerity engines not being fitted with anti-glare shields - the Management Side stated arrangements were in hand for fitting the anti-glare shields to these engines not so fitted.

9th November 1954
No.560 - Staff Side. Request for 04 class engines to be allocated to work Highdyke trains in place of 8 class engines - deferred.

30th September 1955
No.581 - Management Side to bring to notice the irregular use of locomotive coal - the Chairman of the Management Side drew attention to the fact that locomotive coal is for the use of locomotives only and any other use is irregular. Such cases would lead to immediate disciplinary action.

31st January 1956
No.584 - Staff Side, Coaling of Garratt type engines at Frodingham - the complaint was noted and the matter will be investigated.

17th December 1957
No.627 - Management Side, Complaints from the public regarding railwaymen soiling compartments and passengers' clothing by travelling in dirty overalls and/or clothes - the Staff are asked to co-operate in an attempt to avoid future complaints.

24th November 1959
Frodingham Depot; the seniority of links shall be as follows:

Link No.	Name of Link
1	1st Gds/Coal Link ('Highdyke')
2	2nd Gds/Coal Link ('Staveley')
3	Relief Link
4	3rd Gds/Coal Link (Volunteer)
4a	Shed Relief (Drivers and Firemen)
5	1st Pilot (Passed Firemen only)
5a	No.10 Pilot (Passed Firemen only)
6	North Lindsey Light Railway No.1 Pilot
7	Keadby No.2 Pilot (Banker)
8	Shed Link
9	No.5 Pilot (Drivers only)
10	Spare link (16 drivers, 10 firemen)

Firemen will work through the links in seniority order as under:-

Junior Firemen	10
	4a
	4
	2
	1
	3
Senior	5a
Passed	6
Firemen	7
Rotating	8

****

It will be clear that expansion of the links occurred over this period, reflecting an increasingly 'busy' shed. The numbers of turns in each link, hence workings, is not known, though throughout this time there was constant assessment of the link position.

The operation of the banking pilot tender-first stems from complaints from engine crews regarding the prevailing westerly winds blowing coal dust into the engine cabs. There was nothing to be done to stop the winds, but a simple reversal of the direction of banking was instituted and this sufficed until the end of steam.

The preference for the L3 class 2-6-4T engines stems from similar reasoning; it is presumed that certain tender engines were in use as pilots - possibly the J11 'Pom-Poms'. Former L1 class (reclassified L3) Nos.5228 and 5339 were already allocated to Frodingham and within a month of this minute being recorded two further examples, 5273 and 5367, came over from Mexborough.

With regard to the misuse of locomotive coal - while participating on the footplate of the Gunhouse banking pilot about 1960 the author witnessed the throwing overboard of several large chunks of coal down the viaduct embankment to be collected a short time late - for domestic use, no doubt.

The former LMS Garratts commenced working through to Frodingham from about 1955 after the strengthening of a bridge at Swinton, the junction of former LMS metals on to the LNER. The trains worked were ironstone loads from the Midland ore fields. The staff complained on two further occasions over the next 15 months - the first response was a deferral and the 'protest' was noted on the 24th April 1957. Nothing further is recorded with no indication of what the protest entailed. Could the 'coaling with some difficulty while at the shed' have concerned the tubular revolving bunkers of these Garratts - they sometimes stuck and had to be emptied by hand. In addition the Frodingham men had difficulty lining up the coal chute with the openings on the Garratt bunkers.

Reinforced concrete and steel. A detailed view of the medium and its application in the construction of Frodingham shed. North side, west end, 7th July 1960. Photograph R.E. Grimston

Chapter Six

DRIVERS AND DIARIES

The principal wheel arrangements up to the 1880s in terms of numbers were the 0-4-2, 2-4-0 and the 'British Standard 0-6-0'. As demand for power increased along with heavier trains the 0-4-2 and 2-4-0 types merged into the 4-4-0, another 'national standard'. Although single wheelers were utilised specifically on certain traffics they could be regarded as something of an exception. Great Northern Railway coupled engines probably worked excursions and the occasional passenger service between Yorkshire and Grimsby and in so doing exercised the company's running powers over the MSLR between these two localities. After the turn of the century no evidence of GNR train working on the GCR across North Lincolnshire has come to light.

I have made consistent use, through what follows, of records in the form of (sometimes fragmentary) enginemen's diaries for details of locomotives and their working in this area. No Keadby or Frodingham diary in a *complete* form can be traced; there are examples of 'engines only' or of 'work done' but not the two combined. However, much can be gleaned from similar efforts of individuals at Mexborough, Barnetby, Immingham, Grimsby and Lincoln. All these sheds participated in workings associated with the Frodingham area at one time or another. This is excepting the local pilots - though only after, say, 1890-1900 when Keadby's allocation covered all such jobs at Frodingham and at Keadby itself. Prior to this, Grimsby shed was responsible for such work, with much of the shunting performed by goods train engines.

It is fortunate that a record of the first years of Frodingham working has survived in the diary of a Mexborough engineman, by the name of Alvy. During the period 1867-72 the various former South Yorkshire 0-6-0s and similar early MSLR variations had predominated on both goods and passenger work and with increasing numbers of MSLR Class 23 0-6-0s being built, as well as the later Class 18 0-6-0s, more of these types were used locally. Former Great Grimsby & Sheffield Junction Railway 2-4-0s were noted on goods work and an ex-SYR 0-4-2 on passenger. Of the fifty or so locomotives which Mr Alvy worked upon during this period some forty five were 0-6-0s and of these nineteen were the relatively new Class 23; towards 1872 four examples of Class 18 were recorded. The remaining 0-6-0s were of early MSLR origin, or its constituents. Goods services at Keadby and Frodingham worked from Mexborough included the 'Keadby Goods', 'Early Frodingham Goods', 'Frodingham Goods', 'Barnetby Pick-up' and 'Passengers' - doubtless there were others.

William Alvy, engineman of Mexboro' shed.

1871 - firing engine No.176

Feb 6th	Frodingham	On 4.15	Off 5.45	13½hrs
Feb 7th	Grimsby	5.00	8.30	15½hrs
Feb 8th	Frodingham	4.15	9.45	17½hrs
Feb 9th	Frodingham	4.15	5.45	13½hrs
Feb 10th	Frodingham	4.15	6.15	14hrs
Feb 11th	Frodingham	4.15	4.00	11¾hrs
Feb 13th	Keadby Goods	6.30	10.30	16hrs

The Author's first railway photograph. Taken (in short trousers) with a Brownie box camera on a summer evening in 1960, it shows Doncaster K3 No.61847 working the 7.30pm departure from Scunthorpe & Frodingham to Doncaster. Originating at Cleethorpes this train regularly dropped off a fish van at Frodingham. Obviously the local policeman is miles away - he could turn up but blissful ignorance usually ruled. The next photograph I took was a Brush Type 2 on an 'Eccie'- the result was terrible.

45

Top. WD 90719 hauling a load of bolster empties from the sidings at Gunhouse Junction to Frodingham, 5th March 1961. These short trip workings were a regular feature after the laying down of several dead-end sidings at this junction after the Second World War. Due to congestion in the yards at Frodingham such traffic could be stored at Gunhouse until acceptance was received from the Frodingham yard staff. Photograph R.E. Grimston.

Middle. Class 8F 2-8-0 on an 'Eccie' (as we used to say quite some years ago - it meant 'Excursion'). This example shows 48055 hauling a working men's club special from South Elmsall for Cleethorpes. Photograph R.E. Grimston.

Bottom. March 1961 and WD 90598 trundles down the bank towards Gunness with a westbound steel train. It is passing under the Kingsway road bridge of the main Doncaster - Grimsby A18 road. A favourite spot for trainspotters (including yours truly) of the day. Now almost completely overgrown. Photograph R.E. Grimston.

Feb 14th Old Dinting 8.00 9.30 13½hrs
Feb 15th Keadby Gds 6.30 11.30 17hrs
Feb 16th Old Dinting 8.00 11.00 15hrs
Feb 17th Keadby Gds 6.30 11.00 16½hrs
Feb 18th Old Dinting 8.00 10.30 14½hrs

Wages for this period £3-5-0d for a 168¼ hour fortnight. Averages about 12 hours per day, about 4½d per hour.

1876 - driving; engine No.195 except April 29th (No.177) and May 4th (double-headed withNos.174 and 195)

April 24th Frodingham On 2.50 Off 4.30 14hrs
April 25th Frodingham 3.50 6.50 16hrs
April 26th Not required
April 27th Frodingham 6.30 7.30 13hrs
April 28th Not required
April 29th Pilot 3.30 8.00 14½hrs

May 1st Frodingham 6.30 7.00 12½hrs
May 2nd Frodingham 5.00 7.00 14hrs
May 3rd Not required
May 4th Special -BL 7.30 11.00 15½hrs
May 5th Pick Up Barnetby 6.15 7.15 13hrs
May 6th Pick Up Barnetby 6.15 6.45 12½hrs

Notes-
BL = Broughton Lane
Loco No.176 - MSLR Class 23, ex-SYR No.25. 0-6-0 built 1864.
Loco No.177 - MSLR Class 23, ex-SYR No.26. 0-6-0 built 1864.
Loco No.178 - MSLR Class 23, ex-SYR No.23.0-6-0 built 1864.
Loco No.195 - MSLR Class 23, 0-6-0 built 1865.

The titles, 'Keadby Goods', 'Early Frodingham Goods', 'Frodingham Goods', 'Barnetby Pick-up' 'Passengers' and so on were used by Alvy and do not represent MSLR terminology. No extant MSLR working timetable can be traced for this early period; however, the 'Keadby Goods' worked from South Yorkshire up the Keadby Branch and no doubt for goods shipment on to vessels berthed on the Trent bank. 'Early Frodingham Goods' was an early morning departure from Mexborough bound for Frodingham possibly with empties, coal and general goods; 'Frodingham Goods' was similar but later in the morning; the 'Barnetby Pick-Up' from Mexborough ambled along calling at virtually all goods stations picking up and dropping off loads which would then be forwarded at Barnetby after sorting (the reverse would occur for the Barnetby-Mexborough pickup); 'Passengers' denotes just that, of course, but the former South Yorkshire Railway portion of the MSLR was very much a self-contained unit in the Sheffield, Mexborough, Doncaster to Barnetby orbit, with drivers and engines all across the area. Goods loadings would be coal, coal empties, mixed and general with large loads of pig iron with empties back to Frodingham. A very comprehensive survey of locomotive and traffic op-

Grimesthorpe power - the former Midland shed at Sheffield did not often use a 4F 0-6-0 on its Frodingham mineral trains but there is always the exception. 44426 works hard with a coal train up the bank, assisted by O4 63606 on 10th September 1960. Photograph R.E. Grimston.

eration was undertaken on the MSLR during 1886. Below are some extracts from this, bearing out the amount of Frodingham work assigned to Mexboro' and Grimsby sheds. The record was certainly thorough....

Grimsby Goods Engines stabled at Keadby:
March 5th 1886, engine No.156 Driver W. Adsetts, Fireman W. Hock
Sign on 5.00am
Depart Keadby loco shed

Arrive Gunnell 6.00am
Arrive Frodingham with workmans train 6.20am
Shunt 12 hours at Frodingham
Depart Frodingham with ironstone train to Gunness
To Keadby loco shed
Hours worked 15¼
Train miles 8
Empty miles 8½
Shunting miles 76

Total 92

March 5th 1886 Loco No. 173 Driving C. Mawson, Fireman F. Leeson
Shunts Keadby pilot 6.00am to 7.00am
Hours worked 13
Shunting miles 72

March 5th 1886 Loco No. 322 Driver George Freeman, Fireman John Beech
Sign on 6.30am
Depart Keadby loco 7.05am
Arrive Hexthorpe 8.45am
Depart Hexthorpe 9.40am
Arrive Gunness 11.20am
Depart Gunness 12 noon
Arrive Doncaster 2.40pm
Depart Doncaster 3.20pm
Arrive Keadby 4.40pm

Train time 9 hrs 35 mins
Actual time 14 hrs 50 mins
Train miles 82½
Shunting miles 10

Total 92½

Note:
No. 156, ex-SYR No.6. 0-6-0 built 1849.
No. 173, MSLR Class 23, ex-SYR No.22. 0-6-0 built 1862.
No. 322, Class 1B. 0-6-0 built 1874.

Grimsby Goods Engines stabled at Barnetby
March 5th 1886 Loco No. 34 Driver J. Merrills, Fireman C. Goodhand
Sign on 3.45am
Depart Barnetby 4.50am
Arrive Crowle 6.10am
Depart Crowle 6.20am

A Sheffield Midland - Cleethorpes excursion entering Frodingham cutting towards the top of the Gunness bank on 18th June 1961. The Trent Valley can be seen beyond to the west. The engine, Standard 5MT No.73065, would be from Millhouses shed - they were not that common a sight, and were only seen on such workings. Photograph R.E. Grimston.

8F 48061 ambling down Gunness bank through the Frodingham cutting, with down coal empties. The cut down embankment on the left was purchased by the GCR so as to obtain stone and 'muck' in order to embank the nearby viaduct during 1910-12 - see Chapter 1. The date is 16th April 1961. Photograph R.E. Grimston.

Arrive Barnetby	8.00am
Depart Barnetby	9.45am
Arrive Crowle	11.05am
Depart Crowle	11.25am
Arrive Barnetby	12.45pm

and shunts at Barnetby and Frodingham

Train time	7hrs 55mins
Actual time	15hrs 30mins
Train miles	74
Shunting miles	23
Total	97

Note:
No.34, Class 6C 0-6-0 built 1880.

Mexboro Goods Engine Working
March 18th 1886 Loco No. 178 Driver W. Noble, Fireman F. Walker

Sign on	8.50am
Depart Mexboro	9.25am
Arrive Frod.	11.20am
Depart Frod.	12.20pm
Arrive Mexboro	2.15pm
Depart Mexboro	3.15pm
Arrive Frod.	5.10pm
Depart Frod.	6.10pm
Arrive Mexboro	8.05pm

Train time	10hrs 40min
Actual time	17hrs 25min
Train miles	130½

March 8th 1886 Loco No. 488 Driver R. Booth, Fireman J. Atkinson.

Sign on	12.40am

Depart Mexboro	1.10am
Arrive Frod.	3.05am
Depart Frod.	4.00am
Arrive Parkgate	6.20am
Depart Parkgate	7.10am
Arrive Frod.	9.30am
Depart Frod.	10.20am
Arrive Mexboro	12.10pm

Train time	11 hrs
Actual time	13 hrs
Train miles	133

Note:
No.178, MSLR Class 23, ex-SYR No.27. 0-6-0 built 1864.
No.488, Class 6C 0-6-0 built 1882.

The diaries of a Grimsby fireman, one Edward Abey, offer another glimpse at engine use in the 1880s. A driver and his mate were allotted an engine for long periods, and such a crew and engine would be rostered to perform many different duties. These would be of goods as well as passenger. Thus in the example below for July, 1887, with engine No.194 and with driver Oglesby:-

Monday 18th. Passenger special to Ashbury's (Manchester) via Doncaster, 3.30am - 11.30am; return passenger special ex-Ashbury's 9.00pm - 5.45am.
Tuesday 19th. Goods special; two trips to Frodingham for iron, 10.30pm - 8.15am.

Wednesday 20th. Fruit special to Manchester, there was an engine axle broken at Penistone, road blocked eight hours, 10.30pm - 12.00.
Thursday 21st. Goods special, Ardwick (Manchester) to Grimsby, 10.00pm - 9.00am.
Friday 22nd. Goods special to Lincoln and No.125 special back to Cleethorpes, 11.00pm - 9.30am.

The engine used above was a Class 23 0-6-0 built in 1865. As well as the sort of jobs listed there were others, of a routine nature, such as the 'Leeds Goods', 'Hexthorpe Coal' and 'Crowle Goods' along with the various passenger turns out of Grimsby. 'Leeds Goods' would be imported goods from Grimsby Docks bound for the West Riding of Yorkshire; 'Hexthorpe' would be coal from this yard west of Doncaster for export or bunker coal with empties back, whereas 'Crowle Goods' would be local North Lincolnshire traffic to-ing and fro-ing from Grimsby and its docks. Some of Grimsby's passenger turns would naturally serve Frodingham on their way to Doncaster and points west.

The 0-6-0 classes noted for the 1883-92 period included Class 23, 18, 6A, 13 and 25 variants with the more modern 6A and 6C types increasingly evident in the later years. Other engine types commonly listed included Class 15, 1C, 19, 12 and 8 2-4-0s and the Class 6B 4-4-0s. This last example worked the New Holland and (from May 1st 1888,

Cleethorpes) to Manchester passenger service. It appears that by this time the 0-4-2s had been rebuilt, withdrawn or had moved elsewhere. As most of the above-listed classes were utilised on a wide variety of jobs, many would have been found around Frodingham and Keadby.

From about 1890, Keadby took most of its engines from Mexborough and from this time became established more as a 'running shed' with increased staffing, etc. The 6C 0-6-0s, the 'Jumbos', became a feature and remained so until well after the turn of the century, some lasting until the early years of the LNER. Other 0-6-0 classes were represented, for example the Class 9 'Claddies'. When the production series of Class 8A 0-8-0 'Tinys' was built, accommodation was laid down for them at the Keadby site - similarly, the new class 9J 0-6-0 'Pom-Poms', and these two types took over the heavier jobs. Goods tanks of the 0-6-2 arrangement were daily visitors from Staveley and elsewhere, on iron workings. Passenger power before the Great War was in the care of Mexborough-based Class 2 and 2A 4-4-0s with Class 6D and Class 12 2-4-0s from New Holland shed similarly employed. The North American imports, the Class 15 2-6-0s, were familiar on local goods. Engines based at Immingham shed, newly opened from 1912, were more modern, in the main Class 9H and 9J 0-6-0s and Class 8A 0-8-0s. Variety was further widened with Class 8K 2-8-0s soon moving to

Immingham. With the opening of the North Lindsey Light Railway from 1906, it appears that the passenger service to the Humberside villages of Winteringham and Whitton was handled by Keadby 0-6-0 tender and 0-6-2 tank goods engines. From the above it will be evident that Trentside was seeing a selection of both old and new Great Central locomotives but little of the 'main line' passenger engines or mixed traffic 4-6-0s, though such examples could be seen nearby on the east-west route through Gainsborough and Barnetby. Keadby shed, it will have become clear, was a most inconvenient place, squeezed as it was into an awkward site; with its tumbledown structure it was hardly suited to the Frodingham work. Much of this was handled by Mexborough and Immingham-based engines and men and this indeed was to remain the practice, for long after.

With the rationalisation of traffic operation after the 1923 Grouping various foreign engine types were soon evident on Frodingham trains. Pre-Grouping classes during the next two decades included former North Eastern Railway J21 and J27 0-6-0s, Q5 0-8-0s, 2-cylinder B15 and 3-cylinder B16 4-6-0s, as well as the Q6 and Q7 heavy goods 0-8-0s. Ex-Great Northern classes noted were J3, J4 and J6 0-6-0s and K2 Moguls. LNER-built J50 0-6-0Ts were drafted in during the late 1920s in order to strengthen the local pilots. These tanks also worked the

Keadby pilot stints and were given the traditional sobriquet, 'coffee pot'. LNER standard types, J39s and K3s, also appeared on goods work. Ex-GER J17 0-6-0s were further foreigners regularly working into the area, from Whitemoor via the East Lincolnshire line. The foreigners, in accordance with railway tradition everywhere, were not popular with local men; the Doncaster products were deemed fragile and fickle and not as steadfast as Robinson's GCR engines. Firing a GNR narrow firebox, in particular on a 'Long Tom' 0-8-0, was not a welcome task for a Keadby fireman.

George Hutson, a former GCR engineman at Grimsby and Immingham, relates that prior to the opening of Frodingham engine shed much of the traffic eastwards out of Frodingham and a lot of it westbound from the Humber was worked by Immingham engines and men. Below is an example extracted from his 1928 diary, with driver C.Wilson.

20th February 3.55am. Frodingham, on at Immingham, engine No.6574 (O4)
21st February 11.55pm. Frodingham, on at Immingham, engine No.1277 (J39)
22nd February 11.55pm. Frodingham, on at Immingham, engine No.1495 (J39)
23rd February 11.55pm. Special Lincoln, on at Immingham, engine

O4 63692 approaching Frodingham with a Gunhouse Junction - Frodingham transfer coal train on 23rd April 1961. A series of sidings were laid down prior to and after the Second World War at this junction in order to take some of the pressure off the yards and works entrances at Frodingham. When suitable accommodation was found these trains were tripped into the complex of rail sidings. The water tower was formerly situated next to the coaling stage at Dawes Lane sidings; it was relocated during the work on the LNER extensions in the 1920s. The down goods line with the new yard entrances and exits are seen converging on the main line. Photograph R.E. Grimston.

When it was good, it certainly was good. A near pristine B1, 61326 of Doncaster, departing from Scunthorpe & Frodingham with the 5.47pm Cleethorpes - Doncaster passenger. The photographer's long shadow indicates the angle of the early evening sun. 15th August 1960. Photograph R.E. Grimston.

No.6246 (O4)
24th February 11.55pm. Frodingham, on at Immingham, engine No.6622 (O4)
25th February 11.55pm. Frodingham, on at Immingham, engine No.6244 (O4)

Another Immingham man, W. Botham, recorded the following in his daily accounts of 1930:-

17th March 11.10am to 8.40pm Frodingham - Banbury No.6309 (O4), Lincoln - Barnetby No.6304 (O4), light engine No.4308 (D3).
18th March 11.10am to 8.40pm Frodingham - Banbury No.5092 (O4), Lincoln - Barnetby No.5353 (Q4), passenger No.5685 (D7).
19th March 11.10am to 9.00pm Frodingham - Banbury No.6374 (O4), Lincoln - Barnetby No.2692 (J39), passenger No.5685 (D7).
20th March 11.10am to 8.30pm Frodingham - Banbury No.5997 (J11), Lincoln - Barnetby No.6304 (O4), passenger No.5688 (D7).
21st March 11.10am to 8.05pm Frodingham - Banbury No.6298 (O4), Lincoln - Barnetby No.5380 (O4), travel home.
22nd March 11.10am to 7.40pm Frodingham - Banbury No.5092 (Q4),

Pyewipe - Immingham No.1277 (J39).
11th May 10.15pm to 6.15am Frodingham - Woodford No.5152 (Q4), No.6139 (Q4).
12th May 10.15pm to 6.15am Frodingham - Woodford No.6139 (Q4), No.6237 (Q4).
13th May 10.15pm to 7.20am Frodingham - Woodford to Snelland No.6240 (O4), No.6313 (O4).
14th May 10.15pm to 7.40am Frodingham - Woodford to Lincoln No.6282 (O4), home passenger.
15th May 10.15pm to 6.20am Frodingham - Woodford No.6348 (O4), No.5978 (J11).

Both Banbury and Woodford were transfer points to the Great Western for steel trains to south Wales. The Immingham men worked out of Frodingham and were relieved at Lincoln or thereabouts on these trains. In 1931, the following are recorded:-

23rd July 1.49am to 9.49am Immingham - Frodingham No.2368 (B16).
24th July 1.35am to 9.55am Immingham - Frodingham No.6335 (O4).
25th July 1.35am to 12.55pm Immingham - Frodingham No.6224 (O4).

26th July 1.35am to 9.35am Immingham - Frodingham No.5396 (O4).
9.28pm to 6.25am New Clee - Bulcroft, lodge Doncaster No.6046 (J11).
27th July 7.00pm to 4.25am Castle Hills - Immingham No.6177 (Q4).

The Immingham to Frodingham train could have been imported iron ore or return steel empties (steel for export). The trip to South Yorkshire and back would be out with coal empties and return with export or bunker coal.
A further glimpse is given by a page from the 1937 diary of driver Frank Emmitt, again, of Immingham, with fireman F. Coleman-

25th October 2.15am
Frodingham 8 hours No.6349 (O4).
26th October 2.15am
Frodingham 8 hours No.6051 (J11).
27th October 2.15am
Frodingham 8 hours No.6273 (O4), No.6593 (O4).
28th October 3.00am
Frodingham 9 hours 20 minutes No.6497 (O4), No.6051 (J11).
29th October 2.15am
Frodingham 8 hours No.6051 (J11).
30th October 2.15am
Frodingham 8 hours No.5380 (O4), No.5326 (J11).

Passenger traffic was still handled by a mix of pre-1923 classes. Various former GCR 4-4-0s - D6, D7 and D9 - were regular performers, with the occasional 'Director' on the Manchester to Barnetby. Two D6s replaced a pair of ageing D7s at Immingham during the late 1930s with former GNR Class D2 and D3 4-4-0s mixing with the home-grown products. 0-6-0 classes were also noted, J11 and J6 being adequate replacements for 4-4-0s on local passenger and excursion trains. Frodingham in fact possessed an example of a passenger type prior to and after the Second World War - an Ivatt-designed D3, No.2126, allocated from May 1937 and replaced by D2 No.2177 when the former went to Hitchin in November 1938. 2177 left for Doncaster in February 1940 with 2178, another D2, coming to Frodingham at the end of 1945 until withdrawal in July 1947. Principally these locomotives were associated with local passenger work, workmen's trains from Thorne and an evening service to Barnetby, though a 'Pom-Pom' served as often as not.

So it was not all mineral and goods 0-6-0s, 0-8-0s and 2-8-0s. Running-in trips of 4-6-0s out of works on Doncaster-based passenger diagrams further varied the routine - during April 1930, for example, 'Scottish Directors' Nos.6380 and 6400 graced the local services. Streamlined B17 No.2859 EAST ANGLIAN was even recorded, running to Cleethorpes from Doncaster. Other B17s regularly ran the odd sortie on such running-in trials and continued to do so well into British Railways days.

After the Second World War north Lincolnshire became the final home for the GCR Compound 4-4-2s, the Class B3 4-6-0s, as well as some members of the B2 'Sir Sams' and B7s. Consequently a certain air of faded grandeur was evident at Scunthorpe & Frodingham station. This did not last long - the ubiquitous Thompson B1s were coming off the production line and both Doncaster and Immingham used them on local passenger services. By 1950, apart from the odd K2 and K3, this class predominated over all others.

Returning to the Frodingham goods traffic - the Second World War created a sort of managed confusion, with all manner of engines working all types of traffic. According to the LNER *Appendix to the Working Timetable,* nothing much heavier than a 4-6-0 was allowed east of Thorne Junction. The bridges over the canal and road (adjacent to Thorne South station) were less strong than the authorities would like and this restricted heavy engine axle-weights between Thorne Junction (half a mile to the west where the Doncaster - Hull line meets the Frodingham line) and Barnetby. During the war these restraints remained in place but instances were recorded of Gresley V2 2-6-2s travelling through the area.

Soon after the end of the war virtually the whole of the Gresley 2-cylinder O3s were based at Frodingham. Of an allocation of 66 engines there were twenty O3s, twenty-two O4s and eleven J11s as main line goods power. The remainder were J50s and Q1s on local pilot work, plus the solitary D2 No.2178, usually out

of steam on 'Moses Road' at the rear of the shed. By mid-1950 the O3s had gone, replaced by more O4s and half a dozen O2s. After a year or two came the Austerity 2-8-0s; Stanier 8F 2-8-0s also worked in, from deepest Derbyshire and points south, along with the odd Garratt after 1955. Thus the pattern was set until steam's demise. Many other types, in particular former LMS engines, worked into Frodingham, and often through to Cleethorpes on excursion trains. Jubilees, the odd Patriot, Crab 2-6-0s and so on all made their mark on the local scene in addition to the BR classes.

In summary the remaining years of steam saw varying mixes of the following principal classes;- the various divisions of O4, O1, O2 and WD 2-8-0s; K1 and K3 2-6-0s; the B1 4-6-0s; J11 and J39 0-6-0s and the J50 0-6-0T with lesser numbers of 8F 2-8-0s and B16 4-6-0s. Reminiscing with many local retired railwaymen it is Robinson's plodding workhorses, the O4s, that affectionately linger in many a memory. But it was still a long and hard job of work.

Below. The result of a broken coupling on a coke train on the way up Santon Bank during 1956. The location is Appleby station where the signalman had the foresight to divert the runaway into the goods yard, with the results we see here. Unfortunately for the locals, blast furnace coke was not a good burn on open grate fires - the stuff didn't burn hot enough; fortunately, no traffic was waiting or passing at the crossing.

Above. The North Lindsey Light Railway - a 1959 view from the north of Normanby Park sidings with an O4 approaching the north signal box. From here the train will be propelled into the yard, to be taken by works locos to Normanby Park steelworks, a mile or so in the murk on the right. An Ore Mining Branch 'Janus' diesel is pulling ore empties to the Thealby Ironstone Mine further up the branch, on British Railways track. The sidings of the Dragonby Underground Ironstone Mine are visible top left. Photograph J. Oxley.

Below. The Trent Down Sidings (or Trent Yard) area of Frodingham, suitably hazy, around 1960. North Lincoln signal box is to the left/west of the through main lines. Behind this is now located the present coal handling plant. Trent yard itself is mid-distance on the right hand side. Photograph J. Oxley.

Chapter Seven

INWARDS - OUTWARDS

With an improving economic climate from 1934/5, steel production rose accordingly. Increases in capacity were made through the period and a major ironmaking plant was put down just prior to the Second World War at the works of Appleby-Frodingham. (Appleby and Frodingham works had been joined under the United Steel Co. banner from 1917). The very large (for the time) American-inspired blast furnaces and accompanying ancillary plant increased output. These furnaces demanded more coal and more ironstone which was fed to the works through Entrance 'E' - the former Midland Ironstone Branch. In other words, additional coal and coke from South Yorkshire and ironstone from local sources as well as the Midlands were added to the inwards traffic at the New Yard. In addition to these, obviously, were outwards empties and more steel-carrying stock.

Within ten years of the end of war the three iron and steel works expanded output further. Two more very large furnaces were added, at what became South Ironworks at 'App-Frod'. These additions brought about the closure of the cramped original ironmaking site at the Frodingham works opposite the Goods Yard and ironmaking at the old Appleby works was terminated by the mid-1950s. Another steel melting shop (named Frodingham) was laid down at App-Frod with production commencing during 1947. This was additional to the already considerable output from the Appleby melting shop. The four large blast furnaces at South Ironworks were officially termed the 'Four Queens' during 1954 by United Steel management. The individual names were 'Queen Anne', 'Queen Bess', Queen Mary' and 'Queen Victoria' ('Annie', 'Bessie', 'Mary' and 'Viccy' were the local sobriquets) and replaced the more prosaic Nos 9, 10, 11 and 12. By 1948 the iron and steel complex at Frodingham was the largest in the British Empire. All this increased activity generated much more traffic than the railway layout of the 1920/30s could really cope with. Moreover, the railway was always short of staff to operate the yards, as well as run the trains - the principal reasons for this state of affairs were, ironically, the very much higher wages and the regular hours available at the iron and steel works. Shortage of housing was another factor, for the town of Scunthorpe was bursting at the seams as men and their families flocked to the area, to take up employment in the works. The peak years as regards output of steel were the mid-1950s to early 1960s.

Frodingham was not unique in being a combined collection of marshalling yards and private sidings. Similar conditions applied in South Wales, the North East and the Scottish Lowlands but none of these areas approached Frodingham in terms of volume and complexity of operation. The revenue statistics in terms of originating tonnages, receipts and similarly for the immense amounts of coal, coke, ironstone, 'galli' (foreign) ore, limestone, scrap, loaded in and empties out emphasised the fact that Frodingham was, in a commercial and operating sense, in a class of its own.

The yards, however, could not be compared with the likes of Whitemoor, Toton or Healey Mills. These were straightforward marshalling yards and performances could be measured in terms of wagons shunted (per shift, week or whatever.) At Frodingham, a proportion of wagons, being in trainloads, was never shunted, but despatched direct to the various works or entrances for receipt by works shunters, or pushed in by the BR

Sixty years or so old, but still going strong. The reliability of the GC 'Pom-Pom' is testified by their longevity. In July 1960, Frodingham's J11 64395 works a Doncaster goods, a job it would have handled for many years. The local Co-Op siding (serving its coal yard) leaves the up goods in the background. **Photograph R.E. Grimston.**

A detailed, diagrammatic layout of the area's railways, dated about 1958.

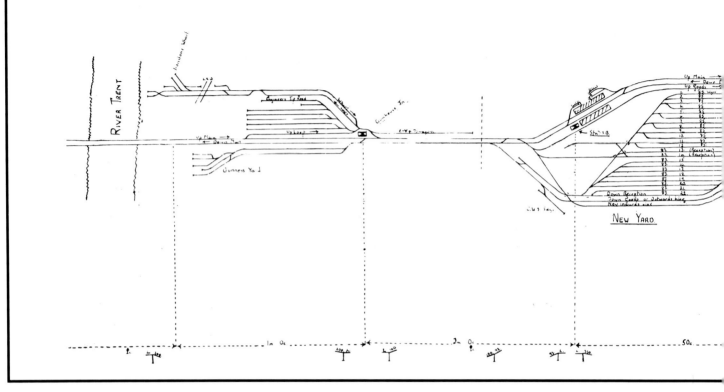

A trainload of pig iron for the Rotherham Works of Steel, Peech & Tozer, behind WD 90063 on 4th March 1961. This was a daily occurrence, for Appleby - Frodingham supplied its sister concern within United Steel with iron for steelmaking. The wagons were a distinctive limy white colour and the train is passing the old station and cripple sidings, adjacent to Alexander Road. Photograph R.E. Grimston.

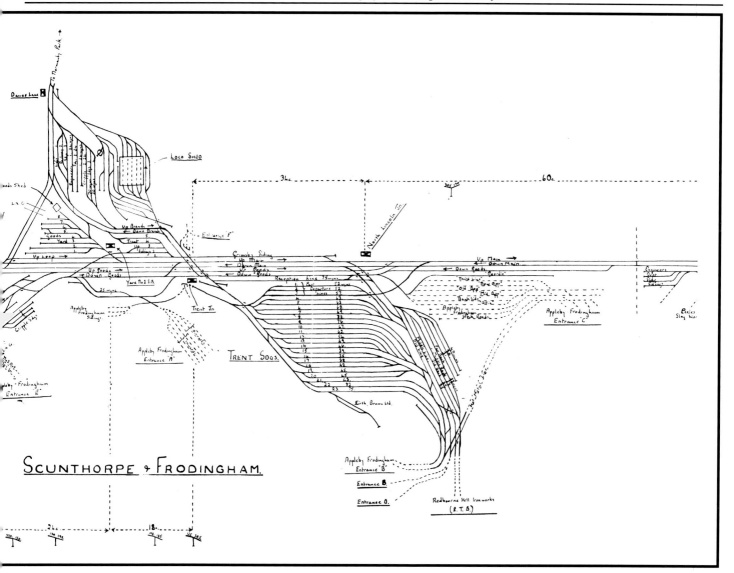

SCUNTHORPE & FRODINGHAM.

8th March 1961, with local O4 63626 acting as one of two Normanby Park pilots, working to Frodingham along the 'Light' Railway at Crosby Mines box. The train consists mainly of empty dolomite containers, ultimately bound for the Hartlepools. This material was used in refractory repairs in the steel furnaces. Photograph R.E. Grimston.

The east end of New Yard, with a WD 2-8-0 pulling out a train of imported ironstone or coal slack, in the early 1960s. The cripple sidings are rear left and the shunters' amenity block is to the right. 'New Frodingham Village', an estate of terraced houses put down for ironstone workers employed by Rowland Winn in the 1870s, is to the rear of the photograph. Photograph R.E. Grimston.

wagons shunted into another siding. This could happen several times before the steel plate wagon ultimately arrived at App-Frod entrance 'B' and was placed for outward loading. Rough traffic for Normanby Park would be shunted over in New Yard, tripped by the Light Railway No.1 or 2 pilots up to Normanby Park sidings, and shunted over there before disappearing up the works branch to Lysaght iron and steel works. Yet again, block loads might be roughly formed up by works shunters down at North Lincoln, to be tidied up by the branch pilot to depart from Frodingham as a trainload, not really being shunted at all. This was an essential and substantial portion of the Frodingham work load.

There was obviously a considerable degree of co-operation between the railway and its clients. Not that the above-mentioned modes of operation did not give rise to conflict at times. Essentially, contact with the steel companies was on two levels - that between the Frodingham Yardmaster and his Assistants and the Works Transport Managers and at a more practical level, between the BR foremen/shunters and the steel works equivalent. The supply of empty steel wagons in timely and sufficient quantities was always potentially a source of friction but not often at a personal level. At the works the problems of local railway management in obtaining sufficient empties were rec-

pilot. Alternatively, they might be 'recessed' awaiting acceptance in a yard siding or on one of the 'running lines' used for such purposes (in particular at weekends) before being delivered by a BR pilot. Many wagons, conversely, would have several shunts, for example, an empty steel plate wagon would arrive at New Yard in a load of 'roughs' (a mixed load) from Doncaster. It would then be shunted out to form part of a collection of plate wagons until required by App-Frod, or the requirement might be for single bolster wagons to App-Frod entrance 'A' and the road would be 'turned over' (a yard phrase) to get the singles and the plate

O4 63626, a pilot working light to Normanby Park sidings - beyond, WD 90284 pulls a train of iron ore for Staveley, from the mines up on the North Lindsey Light. The location is just south of Crosby Mines signal box, with worked out ironstone mines in the background. Photograph R.E. Grimston.

Frodingham O4 No.63595, not far from home with an oil train, passing through Doncaster station on 9th July 1960. Photograph R. E. Grimston.

ognised but deficiencies in the wagon supply could only encourage a gradual changeover to road haulage.

It occasionally happened that the Frodingham yards became full to the point of congestion and this had a 'blocking back' effect into the works, hindering the prompt disposal of empty wagons and outward traffic. More often than not the opposite occurred, however, and the works would appeal to BR to hold traffic back

because they were in turn 'blocked up'. Some easement of this was probably gained through the regulation of inward coking coal in block loads - these came from Durham (there were others from south Yorkshire) and were known as 'convoys'. The Redbourn works of Richard, Thomas & Baldwin Ltd. took most of its coal from the north east and in normal circumstances could only deal with two 'convoys' a day. There was daily contact

between the works and BR - the two protagonists as it were - concerning the acceptance forward from the North Eastern Region, or into Frodingham or into the works. Quite often loads were 'stood back', stabled in the sidings at Stainforth or Gunhouse, with some holding points in Frodingham itself, maybe, waiting acceptance from Redbourn works, where the layout was severely restricted. Better internal capacity at App-Frod and Lysaght meant these two did not require as much attention.

Contact at the physical transfer points was friendly enough but 'blunt'. The works people could change their minds after traffic had been handed over to BR and wagon labels substituted for different destinations; wagons might be shunted off, or on, to make up loads, sometimes without proper notification. This led to unpleasant surprises when the pilot or train crew arrived to take the train away. Harsh words, charges and counter-charges, would result. Generally though, relationships were quite tolerable. In order to get the job done co-operation was the order of the day.

By the mid-1960s the United Steel Co. intended to further increase output at the App-Frod works. The result was a flurry of proposals to modify and expand the yards and the firm's operations at Frodingham. The principal theme was to divert the main line north of the running lines to behind North Lincoln signal box and alter traffic flows within this ex-

Long since gone and no doubt gracing someone's living room wall! These two signs were located on the North Lindsey Light, on the north side of Dawes Lane level crossing. Phillip R. Meyer was the rather ineffectual secretary of the NLLR; real power lay with his brother, Sebastian - the 'Light Railway King of the North' in Dr. Barnett's eyes. By 25th May 1964 it looked as if someone had tried to nick the NLLR sign - one of its bolts has gone. Photograph Alec Swain.

Mrs Elliott, Phyl Jackson, Doreen Goodyear (at back) Blossom (at front) Clarice Girdham (back) Titch Barley (front), Kathy Harrison, Gwen Wolverson, Mrs Hall, Daisy Ellerington, Reg Pinner (Chief Clerk), Mr. Howell (Goods Agent), Mr. Waddilow (Stationmaster, leaving), Mr. Wardell (Relief Stationmaster), Mrs Waddilow, Mr. Selly (Assistant Yardmaster), Mary Johnson, Christine Pridgeon, Betty Ellerington, Jimmy Herron (Foreman), Ted Thompson (Foreman) about 1945. The occasion is a leaving presentation to Mr. Waddilow, stationmaster at Scunthorpe & Frodingham during the mid-1940s. Photograph G. Askew Collection.

panded layout, but there were the old familiar problems over land, and the existing installations could not have coped with the expansion of traffic. Congestion would have 'blocked back' (a familiar phrase at Scunthorpe) into the works, straining relations and contributing further to the trickle away to the roads. To quote a former Frodingham Assistant Yardmaster *'...a background to this was the growing realisation at faraway Liverpool Street that all their fancy exploitation of the 1955 Modernisation had done nothing to help the principal traffic and revenue earning centre of the Eastern Region. We had even been the last (or nearly so) to secure 350hp diesel shunters in place of steam! I recall a visit by an officers' special (the only one in three years) carrying Gerry Fiennes, Henry Johnson, Harold Few etc. which I had to host in the absence of Bill Nock (the Frodingham Yardmaster). Having a 'special relationship' with Gerry Fiennes I took bold advantage of the opportunity to express the disillusionment of the forgotten army at Frodingham and to demonstrate the volume of the business and the archaic equipment we handled it with. I like to think it made an effective impression on the ER management of the time, which*

was of a calibre which appreciated straight talking, and helped the modernisation process along. I recall that I prised out more time to beat their ears, in what was quite a quick visit, by holding their special back to let a steel train out main line, with the acid comment that it earned money whereas their special didn't. Did I push my luck!'

One further quote succinctly puts into focus this relationship between Frodingham and the powers that be; *'.. the traffic machinations at Frodingham were always a source of deep bewilderment to the costing service, commercial negotiators and most other people in the Eastern Region and BR ...'*

At the time of writing (1994) about 80% of steel traffic leaving the steelworks at Scunthorpe is by road....

SHUNTING AND TRIPPING PILOTS, FRODINGHAM c. 1958

No.1 - Shunts West End Trent Down Sidings 22.00 Sunday to 14.00 Sunday. 1 Head Shunter, 2 Shunters.
No.6 - Shunts Trent Low Yard (East End) 22.00 Sunday to 14.00 Sunday. 1 Head

Shunter, 2 Shunters.
Duties rotate 3 weeks each pilot then changeover. Head Shunters: Joe Garrod, Harold Picksley, Arthur Thompson, Len Raynor, George Bonser, Vacancy.
No.2 - Shunts New Yard (Outwards) 22.00 Sunday to 14.00 Sunday. 1 Head Shunter, 2 Shunters.
No.7 - Shunts New Yard (Inwards) 22.00 Sunday to 14.00 Sunday. 1 Head Shunter, 2 Shunters.
Duties rotate 3 weeks each pilot then changeover.
Head Shunters: Fred Royston, George Harris, Les Kirman, George Balmforth, John Pacey, Frank Smith.
No. 3 - Shunts App-Frod. Entrance 'A; and transfers to/from New Yard and Trent, 22.00 Sunday to 14.00 Sunday. 1 Head Shunter, 1 Shunter.
No.5 - Shunts Goods Yard 06.00 Sunday to 22.00 finish Sundays excluded. 1 Head Shunter, 1 Shunter. Head Shunter on duty 10.00 to 06.00. 6 week rotation.
Head Shunters: Charlie Rysdale, Albert Ward, Fred Stones, Ron Pidd, Bill Ellis, Vacancy.
No.4 - Shunts Redbourn and App-Frod. Entrance 'B', 'C' and 'D' from North Lincoln, 22.00 Sunday to 14.00 Sunday. 1

Head Shunter, 1 Shunter.
Head Shunters: Fred Westland, Albert Graves, Charlie Stansfield.
No.8 - Transfers Trent-North Lincoln-New Yard, 22.00 Sunday to 14.00 Sunday. 1 Head Shunter, 1 Shunter.
No.9 - Shunts railway, private owners wagons (of old) and Dawes Lane Cripple Sidings and assists App-Frod. Entrance 'E'. 14.00 Monday to 06.00 Saturday Winter. 22.00 Monday to 06.00 Saturday Summer. 1 Head Shunter, 1 Shunter.
No.10 - Shunts App-Frod. Entrance 'E' and trips to New Yard, 22.00 Sunday to 14.00 Sunday. 1 Head Shunter, 1 Shunter.
Rotation of duties: Head Shunters: Hector Barnes, Tom Sheppard, Stan Beardsall, Charlie Thornton, Edgar Welburn, John Knight, Arthur Sleight, Charlie Oldfield, Harold Clayton.
North Lindsey Light Railway:-
No.1 - Trips Frodingham - Normanby Park and Shunting Normanby Park, 22.00 Sunday to 14.00 Sunday. Trips to Frodingham 05.30 and 12.00, roughs back from New Yard 15.00 and 23.00, tipplers to Crosby Mines 07.00. Guard.
No.2 - Trips and Shunting, 04.00 to 20.00 Mondays to Saturdays. Guard. Moves ironstone ex-Crosby Mine 11.00 and load back, assists Crosby Mine to Staveley if required.
Normanby Park - 3 Head Shunters: Harold Noble, Walter Mason, Alf Barley. 1 Shunter, 22.00 to 06.00 continuous, Walker.
App-Frod. Entrance 'E' Branch - 3 Head Shunters: Jim Duffield, George Clarke, Ernest Streets.
App-Frod. Entrance 'E' - 3 Head Shunters: Stan Wardle, Reg Dent, Maurice Coppinger. 3 Female Shunters.
Rest Day Relief - Head Shunters: D. Harvey, Walter Cale, Vacancy.

SIGNALMEN, FRODINGHAM c.1958
Relief Signalmen - Special Class: Raymond Baker, Reg Wilson. Class 1: Jack Skinner, Charles Richardson. Class 2: Brian Ryder (rest day relief).
Trent Junction - Special Class B: Tom Walton, Eric Wagstaff, George Pratt.
Yard No.1 - Special Class A: Harry Grinnell, Jack Resigh, Robert Kirk.
Yard No. 2 - Class 1: Jack Bayley, Frank Gosling, Fred Jackson.
North Lincoln - Class 2: Jim Toner, Vacancy, Leslie Robinson.
Station - Class 3: Dick Hutchinson, Alex Foster, D.A. Dunham
Dawes Lane - Class 3 - D.C. Danks, Ronald Robinson, G. Lee
Crosby Mines* - Class 3: Ernest Hollingsworth, Vacancy.
Santon - Class 4: Herbert Britcliffe, N.H. Vessey, B. Emmerson.
Weigh Office - Class 4: Walter Shipley, Iris Bush..
Normanby Park North* - Class 4: Frank Green, Cyril Driffill, J. Brown.
Normanby Park South* - Class 4: George

Welsh, Henry Cuthbert, Edith Bell. (North Lindsey Light Railway signal boxes marked * were the home of a number of 'green carders'; that is, semi-invalid staff).

FRODINGHAM YARD STAFF c. 1958
Yardmaster - Bill Nock
Assistant Yardmaster - Jack Mattock, Fred Bell, Eric Hammond
Chief Clerk - Harry Tuffee
Class 3 Clerk - Peter Osborne
Class 4 Clerk - Charlie Standerline.
Telephonists - Helen Nunns, Kath Bell.
Shorthand Typist - ? Jones
Yard Inspectors (train loadings) - Cyril Bell, Jim Davies, Don Warrington.
Inspector Timekeepers - Orriss Mason, George Smith, Eric Nearbert
Yard Inspector (Normanby Park) - Albert Armitage
Yard Foreman - 12 in number including rest day relief. Divided into two links, six working Trent and North Lincoln, 3 weeks each place and five working Yard No.2 and New Yard West End, 3 months each place. No foreman on night duty at Yard No.2.
North Lincoln/Trent - Ralph Snell, Fred Kettleborough, Len Dickinson, Frank Francis, Ernest Boughton, George Bowd.
West End/Yard No.2 - Ron Hoggard, George Whitfield, Cyril Knight, Fred Catchpole, Vacancy.
Rest Day Relief - Reuben Firmage
Acting Foreman - Charlie Stansfield
Signal Lampman - Thomas McLeod
Signal Lampwoman - Gladys Swannell
Signal Lamplad - David Jollands
There was also a porter and some messengers

FRODINGHAM IRON and STEEL WORKS TRAFFIC 1958

John Lysaght's Normanby Park Works:-
Traffic Manager - Mr. Holt
Inward Traffic - Mr. Lawrence
Outward Traffic - Mr. Thomas
General Traffic and Slag - Mr. Sissons
Empty Wagon Requirements - single, double and bogie bolsters, highs and vans
Outward Traffic - billets to Bredbury (Stockport) and Meadow Hall (Sheffield), tinplate to Newport, billets to Cardiff.
Scottish Agriculture Industries and Nitrogen Fertilisers Ltd. were connected to Lysaght and dealt mainly in slag and its by-products.

Richard, Thomas & Baldwin, Redbourn Works:-
Transport Manager - Mr. Nightingale
Assistant - Mr. James
Four Traffic Foremen covered 24 hours, these in contact with BR's North Lincoln foremen.
Empty wagons supplied were mainly single, double and bogie bolsters, boplates and plates. Much of the billets and slabs went to South Wales.

United Steel Co. Appleby-Frodingham Works:-
Transport Manager - Mr. Fowler
Assistants - Mr. Beeby and Mr. Howden
Entrance 'A' - steel out, empty single, double and bogie bolsters, highs and some plate wagons supplied.
Entrance 'B' - supplied with empty plate wagons, trestols, boplates, vans and highs.
Entrance 'C' - loaded steel out.
Entrances 'D' and 'F' - virtually dormant
Entrance 'E' - raw materials in (coal, coke and iron ore from the Midlands)

Firth Brown Ltd
Private siding off No.23 Siding Trent Low Yard
Transport - Mr. Parker

Clugston Cawood
Private siding No.16 Entrance 'E'

SCUNTHORPE & FRODINGHAM Tonnages and Receipts 1955

Forwarded tons (iron, steel and by-products) 2,377,000 tons
Received tons (ironstone, lime, pyrites etc.) 2,810,000 tons
Received coal and coke 2,645,000 tons
Total 7,832,000 tons
These 7.8 million tons (all rail hauled) applied to United Steel Co. Richard Thomas & Baldwins and Station (town) traffic.
Normanby Park Goods Station : John Lysaghts traffic (estimated)
Forwarded 475,000 tons
Received 704,000 tons
Received coal and coke 550,000 tons
Total 1,729,000 tons

Combined total of all iron and steel works plus town traffic:-
7,832,000
1,729,000
9,561,000 tons for 1955

On top of these tonnages hauled inward/outward by BR were substantial tonnages of wayleave (i.e. steelworks traffic using or crossing BR lines e.g. North Lindsey Light) free-hauled railway contract, etc. traffic on which no receipts arose, including slag ballast for permanent way purposes. Hence, approximately 10 million tons of all material hauled by British Railways during 1955 in the Scunthorpe & Frodingham area.

Originating receipts (1955)
Scunthorpe £2,787,000
Normanby Park £508,000
Total £3,295.000
Wages outlay - approximately £400,000. This excluded all Locomotive Department wages and salaries. (Source former Goods Agent, Scunthorpe.)

Above. Scunthorpe station, 1st July 1982 - the 12.45pm Manchester Piccadilly to Cleethorpes trans-Pennine dmu, with E51956 leading. Photograph A. Swain.

Below. Loads vary! This one is a single load of billets heading west out of Scunthorpe. The layout is now much simplified compared with steam days and a class 37 can be seen in the former goods yard - a pair of these types work to and fro with coal trains from these sidings to the coal handling plant. Scunthorpe power box is on the right. 13th April 1995. Photograph B. Longbone.

Chapter Eight

'YET MORE CHANGES'

The table illustrates the quantities of raw materials to, from and within the Frodingham iron and steel conglomerate from the late-1930s through to the 1970s. As far as railway operation is concerned, certain points become clear. There is the somewhat rapid decline of local ore production from the late 1960s, coupled with the elimination of all iron ore movement from the Northamptonshire fields. The deficiency was, of course, taken up by foreign ore through Immingham Docks, in considerable volume. As this imported ore was much higher in iron content than local or Northamptonshire material, a smaller quantity was required to produce the same (or an increased) amount of pig iron. Coal suffered a steady decline due to more efficient blast furnace operation. In summary, there is now far less material to move by rail and running parallel with this is a steady erosion of outgoing steel traffic, from rail to road. A rough estimate for the present (1992-93) gives *only about 20%* of steel leaving by rail.... Virtually all coal and iron ore is moved by rail but the bulk of coal, incredibly, now comes from abroad.

A few notes on the iron and steel works expansion can add flesh to the above figures - the period after the war saw the industry nationalised - though not for long, the exception of Richard, Thomas & Baldwins at Redbourn remaining in Government hands. In addition, large projects were undertaken to improve postwar production. In 1947 the Appleby-Frodingham works installed a large new melting shop (closing the old original of 1890) and modernised the rolling mill. Seven years later two very large blast furnaces were built to replace and improve upon older plant at the same company. At the Redbourn works of RTB the blast furnaces were modernised and a new battery of coke ovens constructed. This works was busy supplying re-rollers in the Midlands, Sheffield and south Wales with billets. The Monks Hall works at Warrington was another customer and slabs were also sent to Ebbw Vale, for the strip mill located there. Traffic for this had commenced in the 1930s and also included other varieties of semi-finished steel. Finally, at Normanby Park, new coke ovens, one new blast furnace and a new steel furnace were laid down. From the mid-1950s to about 1960 production was at peak volumes and tonnages.

The *Anchor Project,* a completely new steelmaking plant (using high volumes of oxygen) with rolling facilities, came on stream in 1973. Recession soon caught up with the Redbourn and Normanby Park works and, not to put too fine a point on it, they have been reduced to rubble, leaving Anchor and the rump of Appleby-Frodingham to maintain production.

All the above-noted changes have directly affected railway operations. The days of steam power had witnessed an endless series of trains night and day, from the east and west, into Frodingham - all moving into the choked-up yards and sidings of British Railways and the works with the official *Rules and Regulations* stretched to suit local circumstances. The locomotive department was under pressure, offering much poorer wages and less regular hours than the steel industry, but the system somehow worked, and the accounts of the Eastern Region looked healthy indeed. These healthy levels of work were maintained for the first ten or so years of dieselisation after 1965 but changes in raw material flows altered traffic movements. With reliance on richer, foreign iron ore the importance of the deepwater channel in the Humber estuary attained a crucial note - large carriers cross the North Sea from the Europort complex in the Netherlands, delivering iron ore to the Humber bank. Even larger carriers deliver mammoth tonnages of iron ore to Europort from various worldwide sources (South America, Canada and elsewhere.). Transfer is undertaken off-shore with the ore, suitably crushed, pelletised and otherwise concentrated, and loaded on to the trainload units which travel the twenty or so miles to Santon Ore Terminal at Frodingham, some eight-twelve times daily (it depends on the vessels unloading). A similar method is used for the importation and transfer of coal from various places abroad, again long hauls (e.g. Australia) in bulk carriers. Prior to this, merry-go-round coal was taken through to Frodingham from various coal fields in the UK. Thus varying quantities of coal were blended to produce good quality blast furnace coke.

The locomotives commonly associated with such traffics were, and still are, the class 56 and type 60 diesels. Under pressure from British Steel plc there is a quick turnround from the arrival of the loaded coal train to the departure of the empties at the coal handling plant. This is located north-west of the main through lines behind where North Lincoln signal box used to stand. Trent Yard is a shadow of its former chaotic glory with just a few sidings in use. Bulk steel leaving by rail is despatched from Anchor exchange sidings, from where steel empties are fed in from the Anchor works by shunters of British Steel. Some three trains per day of billets and other items are regularly forwarded to Masboro' (Rotherham) along with the odd special. In addition, there are a few services per day calling in at Trent, dropping off/picking up steel and then proceeding to all points north (Teeside) or points south-west (the Midlands, Cardiff). Steel traffic also exits the App-Frod site over the 'bottleneck' but in very much lesser quantities than a couple of decades ago. Compared with former periods it is a sorry affair.

The BR layout at Frodingham was modernised (and rationalised) during the early 1970s. Power signalling was installed with a control signal box erected adjacent to the site of the original 1866 station. 'New Yard' was designated 'West Yard' at this time but closed down some twenty years later. When modernised this yard was converted to hump operation along with Dowty wagon retarders, but 'wagonload' goods have virtually disappeared along with the requirement for this yard. Entrance 'E', the former extremely busy conduit of coke and iron ore to the ironworks of App-Frod, is now pulled up.

All of this reflects recessionary changes in the local iron and steel industry over the last two decades. As to the

Year	Frodingham stone to blast furnaces	Northants. stone to Frodingham	Foreign ore to Frodingham	Total	Coal used	Total material used in making iron
1938	2351	736	105	3193	-	-
1950	2574	1537	187	4299	-	-
1954	3871	1722	-	-	2520	5047
1958	4298	2142	-	-	2326	5833
1961	5243	2513	222	7756	2763	6490
1965	5076	3307	-	-	2666	6568
1969	4421	3344	1132	8897	-	-
1974	1220	0	2470	3690	-	-

Raw material movements at Frodingham - all figures in 1000s of tons.

- indicates quantity not known

locomotives and their drivers - Immingham is now the 'local' depot and together with Thornaby serves most railway needs. All pilots have gone from Frodingham and train engines perform their own shunting. There are very much fewer of these goods and mineral trains per day, though they are far heavier and with more horsepower up front. Whereas upwards of 200 trains of all types were booked each weekday, now the total is a fraction of this. Oil trains out of Immingham are a common sight heading westwards through Frodingham with long trainloads of 100 tonne tanks hauled by class 60s. Two trains per day arrived from Manchester for some months during 1994; hauled by Class 60s they slowly proceeded up the North Lindsey Light to empty wagons of household waste into Roxby Mine. In addition, waste still goes to the same site from the Tioxide plant on the Humber Bank. What would have been a most unusual sight not so long ago is now commonplace - steel trains working through Frodingham in transit to/from destinations in Europe and elsewhere in the UK. Again, these trains utilise the Humber ports. The situation regarding the local train drivers mirrors the above - only a handful are left with some travelling to other booking-on points away from the local area. The diesel servicing depot, opened in 1966, is now closed.

Trying hard to be positive, however, it must be stated that the passenger service is now more frequent than it has ever

been, no doubt reflecting changing priorities. Scunthorpe station is now on the Regional Railways North-East map and has been suitably refurbished. But it is a pretty dismal affair when compared with the scene a generation ago.

What will occur in another generation ...?

Above. A class 158 dmu on its way to Cleethorpes with a class 60 running light on the down side, at Scunthorpe station on 13th April 1995. Photograph B. Longbone.

15th February 1995 and a class 56 heads for the Humber Bank with the empty waste train returning to the tioxide works. The train has come off the North Lindsey Light where the waste, in addition to choice stuff from the Manchester area (now ceased) is filling former ironstone holes-in-the-ground. The coal sidings on the site of the old goods yard are evident in the foreground. Photograph B. Longbone.

Above. A Cleethorpes-bound class 158 passing the coal sidings at Scunthorpe on 15th February 1995. The mammoth coal storage bunkers at the coal handling plant are in the distance, framed through the rebuilt Brigg Road bridge (formerly viaduct). Photograph B. Longbone.

Below. Only 8 years ago but vastly changed by 1995. The yard is now derelict and no more will the sounds of shunting persist around the clock. This is a view looking across West Yard (the former New Yard) with a couple of brakes at the end of a kip and a Brush Class 31 passing on the main line, with a Cleethorpes to Manchester four coach passenger train. This, by the way, was lovely stock to be travelling in - acres of leg room. Photograph D. Jackson.

Above. A late 1950s view of the Redbourn Iron and Steelworks of Richard, Thomas & Baldwins Ltd. - the author spent ten happy years working here. The lines crossing the picture run south (to the right) from Bottleneck Junction and Trent Yard. In the foreground are the coke ovens (site of the former North Lincolnshire Iron Co. until the Depression) and the plate mills of the Appleby-Frodingham concern. Left to right are coke ovens, rolling mill, melting shop, scrap bay (where bits of Gresley A3 Pacifics were seen in the 1960s), blast furnaces and iron ore preparation plant behind. Slag pits on the right. A very cramped site with wagon space at a premium. The railway had to store inwards wagons for Redbourn at Trent Yard more often than not. The railway to Barnetby curves away to the left, descending Santon Bank. The site of Redbourn is now - a tip.

Below. The engine shed at the Redbourn Works of Richard, Thomas & Baldwins during June 1958. Engines noted were No.21, a Hudswell Clarke of 1922, on the back line and No.28, a Hunslet of 1951. The ingot soaking bay building is to the right, leading to the rolling mill behind. A works steam crane stands alongside. It was 66 steep steps, incidentally, to the top of the water tank on the mill roof (left) every Friday morning, to read the water meter. Photograph J.R. Bonser.

Chapter Nine

'WHERE THERE'S MUCK...

Finally a chapter touching on rail way matters in the various iron and steel works themselves; with constant internal transfers, the tonnage on the move reached formidable levels.

An integrated iron and steel plant possessed its own internal railway network and organisation - repair, maintenance, permanent way, locomotives and wagons, even rudimentary signalling - and staff in numbers to suit. As a result there eventually arose three such works-based locomotive fleets, together with all their accompanying buildings, equipment and plant. Beyond this there were the local ironstone workings, often some distance off, where each of these three works ran a series of excavations. This resulted in an extensive and widespread layout of lines connecting the mines and the consuming sites.

This of course, is to jump ahead many years. Prior to the Great War, with six iron-producing works within the area, the degree of production was not so high and mining was both less extensive and more diverse. From the earliest years until after the Second World War a major player in feeding this local stone to smelters was the Frodingham Ironstone Mines Co. While Rowland Winn was leasing off portions of his estate to the iron smelters he stipulated that his company, the FIM, would mine the ore, grade and supply it to the works. This involved the aforesaid Appleby Iron Co., the Redbourn Hill Iron & Coal Co., the North Lincolnshire Iron Co. and the Lincolnshire Iron Smelting Co. However, the two earliest works of the Trent Iron Co. and the Frodingham Iron Co. obtained the ore themselves. The FIMCo. possessed a fleet of locomotives and, in addition, its wagons left the area loaded with ironstone to be forwarded by the MSLR/GCR for smelting away from Frodingham. Being extremely cheap to mine the stone could bear the extra haulage cost.

There were also several mines along the North Lindsey Light Railway, worked by companies from outside Frodingham. Walter Scott Ltd., of Leeds and the Sheepbridge Iron Co. of Chesterfield amongst others, operated mines, each with rudimentary layouts.

The literature relating to the works transport systems is decidedly thin. Of the three fully integrated works that of Appleby-Frodingham was the only one to document and place in the public realm details relating to its railway operation (in the *Journal* of the Iron & Steel Institute and *The Locomotive*). Like many aspects of life it boils down to one enterprising individual, which brings into prominence E.R.S. Watkin, the traffic manager at App-Frod from the mid-1930s until 1954. Through articles written for the *Appleby-Frodingham Record* and a paper for the JISI in 1953 much can be gleaned of the App-Frod system. Unfortunately a similar state of affairs did not apply in the case of the Redbourn works of Richard, Thomas & Baldwins and the Normanby Park Works of John Lysaght.

The location of the Redbourn Works was severely restricted, with limited storage of wagons - it was closely

The sun's shadows suggest it's the day men (7.30am-4.00pm) going home from South Ironworks on their push-bikes. An 'intermediate' or 'medium' range works tank engine stands in between duties in front of a set of Cowper regenerative stoves - these heated the air up to a high temperature before it was blown into the adjoining blast furnaces. The heat was derived from blast furnace gas burning at the base, thus heating up the organised mass of bricks contained inside. These gave up their heat to the air admitted later - and so on through the cycle. The tank engine is on slag duty - witness the slag pots under the furnace. 'Queen Mary' is the nearest, then 'Bess', 'Anne' and 'Vic' off picture. Taken about 1950. Photograph British Steel PLC.

Crew and foreman (trilby = badge of office) with REDBOURN No.14, posing near the Bottleneck Junction bridge over Dawes Lane. The engine was withdrawn one year after the photograph was taken, during 1959, some 40 years after it was purchased new from Hudswell Clarke. Photograph J.R. Bonser.

bounded on all four sides by App-Frod or mines associated with the latter. App-Frod itself was a sprawling giant and due to the historical background as two separate firms and its subsequent growth (for a time there were three separate blast furnace sites on the App-Frod works) not a great deal could be done to limit relatively long and expensive hauls. The Normanby Park Works, however, was laid down in 1910 on a 'green field' site unencumbered with exhausted ironstone workings - these could play havoc, making for fierce gradients at some locations and increasing the cost and difficulty of working.

The sprawling nature of the App-Frod works have lead to the provision of no less than five 'entrances' - A B C D and E, through which material could be worked to and from the outside world. 'A' was the old Frodingham entrance but in 1953 was the point from which structural steel from the Heavy Section Mill was despatched. Entrance 'B' served the Appleby Steel Works (melting shop and plate mill) along with the new Frodingham melting shop from 1947 onwards. The former Appleby Iron Works (titled North Iron Works by this time) was reached by Entrance 'C'. Entrance 'D' fed

coal to the coke ovens and, finally, Entrance 'E' fed coke and Northants iron ore to South Iron Works (1939 on). This latter entrance was the former Midland Ironstone Siding and branch which led to ore mines on Brumby Common to the east of the town. Redbourn Works lay opposite App-Frod but utilised rails over the 'bottleneck' bridge at Dawes Lane, which came out of Trent Yard. Normanby Park Works were simply connected to the NLLR; Normanby Park Sidings formed the buffer between British Railways and the works themselves.

The local, 'limey' (referring to its lime, or carbonate content) ore at 20-22% iron, served 60% of the App-Frod blast furnace requirements - known as the 'charge'. This was delivered from the mines to the works by means of the 'Ore Mining Branch' (branch in the sense of a sector of the business, not a branch *line*); this was the United Steel Co.'s local ore mining transport system, formed during 1948-53 after absorbing the lines of the FIMCo., the Santon Ironstone Mining Co. and that of the Appleby-Frodingham Iron & Steel Co. under one banner. Northamptonshire ore incidentally, from the Grantham and Melton Mowbray areas, contained 30-33% iron. The other principal ingredient for making iron at App-Frod was coal for the coke ovens on site and already-processed 'bought coke', mainly from south Yorkshire. A principal feature was the inwards and internal movement of low grade traffic (ironstone, coke and slag); with a high proportion of 24cwt (1.2 tons) of slag produced per ton of iron, large quantities had to be disposed on to ever-increasing mountains of cooled slag. At the time it was ideal for ballast and in some cases (with its high phosphorus content) fertiliser - and breeze blocks too, after treatment. Molten slag was transported in cast iron, unlined, ladles but 'hot metal' was carried in refractory (heat resistant) bricklined ladles - hot ingots, each up to 20 tons in weight, were moved in trains of ingot cars. Of the net wagon loads hauled, inward, outward and internal traffic, tonnage was nearly 300,000 per week; of this total approximately 100,000 tons was of ironworks materials with 65,000 tons of hot metal, slag and ingots per week. Weekly inward tonnage was of the order of 75,000 tons with outward steel totalling 25,000 tons. To move all this local and internal traffic there were about 1,800 wagons available at App-Frod. 900 were ore and coke wagons and 600 general internal wagons, the remaining 300 comprising ladles or ingot cars. However, by the 1950s internal haulage was being reduced through the use of belt conveyors, with coke from the ovens and iron ore transported through the crushing, screening, blending, drying and sintering processes by conveyors. In the steel making and finishing processes overhead cranes and roller roads reduced rail

1968 and REDBOURN No.25, a Hunslet of 1944, in a siding of the works engine shed. The melting shop building is behind and, as part of the continual safety drive, various designs of 'toe-tectors' are displayed in a case on the wall. Loco boiler water treatment was attempted at Redbourn, with briquettes dropped into the tubular water tank. Climbing up with a bucketful was one of my routines for a while. A good clean up seems to be required.

John Lysaght's Ltd Peckett No.22 of 1945; the firm had strong links with Peckett's of Bristol. There was a degree of lining out on this and other Lysaght's engines. The locomotive was actually put together in the local workshops from parts supplied by Peckett's. Photograph British Steel PLC.

movement still further. The 1951 weekly total wagon movements numbered 33,530 and the total railway mileage in the App-Frod works for June 1951 totalled 99.2, of which just over half were 'running' routes. The difference was made up of 17 classes of inward sidings, four sets of outward sidings and nearly 20 miles of internal sidings. All this was encompassed within a layout of 1,700 acres.

Given such prodigious tonnages, always on the move within a busy but relatively small area, derailments were relatively few. Take 1951:-

Fault	Weekly Average
Tracks or points	3.0
Rolling stock	1.4
Shuntering* or lock buffering	5.5
Loading, slag tipping, slag or other material on track	5.2
Unknown	1.6
Total	16.7

Local term, reflecting the high degree of bashing and minor damage inflicted on the wagons. The works shunting was often not as delicate as on BR...

Crossings on works railways were avoided if possible as they were sources of derailments - the idea was to keep the layout as simple as possible. In such industrial circumstances, complete, interlocked signalling is unnecessary and impracticable. Usually drivers (in the 1950s that is) relied on their attention to and familiarity with their surroundings; they used whistle codes for certain movements and hand, lamp or whistle signs from their shunters. At App-Frod traffic continued under this system by day and night and ran at '95% of normal' even in foggy conditions. 'Calling on' and lights were used, and there was an extensive system of lighting throughout the works.

With regard to the fleets of locomotives utilised by the various works little but a general summary will serve here. In the early years not all haulage was by steam power. A couple of photographs (too poor for reproduction) survive showing that horses were used to haul slag away from the blast furnaces during the years up to about 1880 - the practice then was to allow the slag to solidify inside small wooden blocks and it was these small cooled lumps of slag that were carried away on rail-mounted cars by the long-suffering horse.

At the end of the Second World War there were 63 engines at App-Frod but changes in operation and maintenance had reduced the total to 57 by 1951, including two of an obsolescent type stored dead. The 55 working steam locomotives were of three main types, all 6-coupled outside cylinder tanks. The 'light' type

Crew Jack Clark and Fred Hudson with John Lysaght Slag loco No.5 - built in 1912 and still going strong some 46 years later, with two tone livery. Photograph J.R. Bonser.

Hudswell Clarke MARY and FRANCES, both 1953 products and out of use when this photograph was taken in May 1964. Construction work for the new LD/AC steelmaking shop is going on to the right. The gas or steam main behind the loco has a wonderful support system. Photograph A. Swain.

were mainly used at the North Iron Works (i.e. the old Appleby site where gantry loads were restricted) and for level shunting in the Frodingham Works mill area. The 'heavy' type was introduced for 'uphill' traffic in 1921 and for wider use during 1934. This 'uphill' reference derives from the fact that the works were on higher ground than the ore mines. The 'medium' version was introduced from

1936 and proved more adaptable, and fully adequate for a wide range of uses. All the post-war additions to the steam fleet at App-Frod were of this type *(see table opposite)*. In 1951 operations were based on 43 locomotive duties of which six were day work, five 2-shift operation and 32 3-shift, round the clock turns. These duties were mainly based on location - melting shop, rolling mill or what-

ever. Light overhauls were undertaken after 12-18 months in service with the heavier repairs performed at 24-30 months. The locomotive crew was a driver plus shunter with the latter, after 12 years service, becoming a driver.

Details as to specific designs and other factual data of the various engines will not be elaborated, suffice to say that many private locomotive builders were represented at one time or another. Firms such as Manning Wardle, Wilson's, Andrew Barclay, Peckett's, Hudswell Clarke, Hawthorn, Hunslet and the Yorkshire Engine Co. amongst others were used. In addition, smaller numbers (often lone examples) were present in the ironstone mining fleets.

A systematic survey of the locomotives used on the ironstone mines, iron and steel works at Frodingham, from the earliest days up to modern times, would be too lengthy by far for this general account. Rather, I've substituted a series of 'biographical snapshots' which reflect the diverse origins and types of locomotives involved. Several hundred worked locally at one time or another and a full account would present many difficulties, not least of space. One pitfall (among many) is the renumbering system, for when a vintage engine was replaced the new one frequently took the same number. In addition, the names of many engines are lost to obscurity and would be difficult to trace. Published listings, however worthy, do have their deficiencies - it has to be said that the history of industrial locomotives has not been examined to the degree enjoyed by the public railways of this coun-

Appleby-Frodingham Works - the largest of the trio of Frodingham integrated works, in a south-west wind, in the 1960s. In the foreground are the stockyards for the heavy section mill (off picture to right). Behind these is the Appleby open hearth steel melting shop ('Nine Chimneys Row') and immediately beyond that and to the left is Appleby Plate Rolling mill. The three tall chimneys beyond betray the coke ovens. At right background are the ironworks Four Queens, 'Mary', 'Bessie', 'Anne' and 'Vic', with the four stacks of Frodingham open hearth steel melting shop in front of them.

Simplified Summary, App-Frod locomotives, 1951				
	Light	**Medium**	**Heavy**	
Number available	1	13	32	2	7
Date built	1910	1917-40	1936-51	1921-27	1934-38
Cylinders	16x24	15x22	16x24	18x24	18x24
Wheel dia. in.	45	41	44	48	44
Tractive effort, lb at 75%	18,432	16,299	18,851	21,870	23,858
Weight full	41	35	50	54	60

try. The subject has been neglected in past years and the material for an appraisal is often not now available.

The local locos were tanks of one form or another for reasons of initial cost and the short distances involved. Nevertheless there was a bewildering array of designs, often rebuilt, adding greatly to the variety of the local railway scene. Moreover the locomotives purchased by a particular concern were not always new - quite often they were second (or third) hand, usually going cheap, with more work to be squeezed from them for further years. In principle they could be kept working almost indefinitely; it was such matters as availability and the price of coal which reduced their flexibility as com-

pared with diesels.

A typical story concerns the Redbourn Works. No.39 was a G6 0-6-0T built at the Nine Elms (London) works of the London and South Western Railway in 1894, for short distance passenger working, and renumbered 237 on Grouping in 1923. Its main line life was terminated with the aid of a V1 flying bomb during World War II and it was written off for scrap by the Southern. It ended up in this condition at George Cohen's yard at Newport in South Wales from where it was brought by Richard, Thomas & Baldwins in 1949. Somehow it was moved to the company's Redbourn works, to be rebuilt. Its principal job was at the despatch end of the rolling mill, shunting empties in and loaded steel out. It was withdrawn in 1958 and no doubt cut up on site though in its dotage was photographed relatively frequently - due to its exotic origins and its *Bournemouth* shed plate, in place on the smokebox! But the question remains, if

put to one side after being bombed during the Second World War for scrap, how did it get the Bournemouth *BR* shed plate? As intimated above, problems do arise....

Redbourn No.6 was another 0-6-0 side tank, built in 1913 by Hawthorn Leslie to a standard design with a maker's number of 3927. It was originally supplied to the Richard & Co.'s works at Ebbw Vale but came up to Redbourn sometime in the mid-1930s. Its main area of operation was on two shift working on the coke ovens. It was withdrawn during 1958.

Redbourn No.40 was unique in the Frodingham area, an example of that relatively rare breed, a fireless locomotive. It was built in 1954 by Andrew Barclay (No.2349) of Kilmarnock and was an example of the firm's standard design. Its work at Redbourn resulted from the extensions to the open hearth steel melting shop during the mid-1950s, and it was employed on hot metal transfer from the mixer furnace, where molten pig iron was stored after being transported from the blast furnaces and in which molten iron of continuously differing specification was 'mixed' to provide a consistent feed to the steel furnaces. This involved only about 70 yards of track, to the charging stage of the adjacent melting shop. Inside the melting shop, under one roof, a conventional locomotive producing exhaust would have obscured the overhead crane drivers' vision. No.40 never worked be-

On the slopes of the volcano. A splendid view of an App-Frod engine 'teeming' (tipping) molten slag (1,000°C +) at the Frodingham Works. When it had been raining heavily, with water lying around, fast legs were necessary. The slag bogies are of the powered variety. Photograph British Steel PLC.

To replace several repair shops dotted about, a central engineering workshop was constructed for Appleby-Frodingham in the mid-1950s. Major repairs and minor construction work was undertaken, with the full panoply of lathes, drills, and other machine tools. This is the loco repair section (for upwards of 50-55 locos) in the late 1950s, with four steam engines and a 'Janus' diesel. Similar establishments along with attendant loco repair shops appeared soon after at Normanby Park and Redbourn Works.

yond these limits, except to go for repairs or attention. A simple 0-4-0, it had medium pressure 150psi steam fed into the reservoir tank 'as required' after a certain number of to and fro trips. It lasted as long as the melting shop - that is, until the new Anchor site came on stream during the 1973/74 and was subsequently scrapped.

The works of John Lysaght at Normanby Park opened from 1910 and No.22 was an outside cylinder 0-6-0ST from Peckett of Bristol, supplied in the form of parts, erected on site between 1910 and 1912. It was principally employed on slag traffic which in later years went to the nearby Tarmac Plant, for roadstone purposes. 22 was withdrawn during 1961.

Another Lysaght's oddity was No.7, an 3ft gauge 0-4-0ST built by Peckett in 1913 for the ingot traffic within the open hearth steel melting shop. When first laid down the ingots were transported between the steel furnaces and the rolling mill on a self-contained narrow gauge system within the works and a number of tank engines were purchased for use thereon. When the melting shop was redeveloped in the early 1950s this narrow gauge system was abolished and No.7 transferred in June 1952 to United Steel's Cottesmore ironstone mines in Rutland. This line closed in 1957 and it is assumed that No.7 was scrapped as a result. John Lysaght's No.13 was yet another Peckett engine (Peckett's was a 'sister' company) built in 1915 as an 0-6-0ST and used on the old

mines route from Dragonby. It was rebuilt in the late 1940s for hauling heavy ironstone traffic.

To turn now to the Appleby-Frodingham works - prior to 1934 the Appleby and Frodingham sites within the United Steel Co. combine were distinct and possessed their own fleets of works locomotives. After 1934 a process of rationalisation and standardisation (to a degree) took place due, in the main, to E.S. Watkins, the Traffic Manager. He classified all the engines into 'light', 'medium' and 'heavy' grades of work and set about renewing and updating those in the latter two categories. He soon found, however, that the 'medium' engines could do all but the heaviest of the 'heavy' work and more of this middle range were introduced, leaving the really 'heavy' engines to the high tonnage ironstone traffic from the nearby mines. No.39 was built by Robert Stephenson & Hawthorn in 1938 as one of the 'medium' standards with two outside cylinders of 16in diameter by 24in stroke, with saddle tanks and 3ft 8in diameter coupled wheels. This was the locomotive that toppled down the Brigg Road slag bank close to Ashby Ville in 1953. It was soon back in service but was sold in 1961 to the National Coal Board from where it moved to the Foxfield Light Railway in Staffordshire.

No.52 was an example of a 'heavy' engine; these had 18in diameter cylinders but with the same stroke as the 'mediums'. Another 0-6-0T, No.52 had come from Robert Stephenson & Hawthorn in

1938. It worked iron ore traffic from Santon, Dawes Lane and Yarborough mines and was also used for cold ingot transfer traffic at the Frodingham melting shop. It was withdrawn in 1964 replaced, like others, by 'Janus' diesels.

No.11 was built in 1952 (notice the oddities of dates and numbers) by the Yorkshire Engine Co. (part of the United Steel family, to which Watkins was soon to move). The engine was a further development of the Robert Stephenson & Hawthorn 'medium' standard from the period before World War II. It served as test bed in January/February of 1955, when flangeless wheels were fitted on the driving (centre) axle; not for long, for flanged wheels were refitted a month later. Like all the 'medium' tanks, it had 16in diameter cylinders with 24in stroke and 3ft 8in wheels. Along with No.52 above, it was taken out of use during 1964.

Ore Mining Branch locomotives in the early years were a mixed bunch, of the old and ancient. Lord St. Oswald's mining concern, the Frodingham Ironstone Mines Co., had a venerable collection, often so rebuilt as to be unrecognisable from the original state. OMB No.2 was a Manning Wardle 0-6-0 of 1913 and under the guise of OMB operation was often employed on iron ore transfer to Crosby Loading Dock.

Lastly, a reference to the well-known and often photographed 'Beauchamp' (no number). Belonging to the Midland Ironstone Co., it was built by Manning Wardle in 1918 and found in